Social Security:
Simple & Smart

Social Security:
Simple & Smart

A series of simple and easy-to-understand fact
sheets that tell you everything you need to know
about Social Security

Tom Margenau

Creators Publishing
Hermosa Beach, CA

SOCIAL SECURITY: SIMPLE & SMART
Copyright © 2020 TOM MARGENAU

Cover art by Kelly Evans

CREATORS PUBLISHING
737 3rd St
Hermosa Beach, CA 90254
310-337-7003

Library of Congress Control Number: 2020950128
ISBN (print): 978-1-949673-50-0
ISBN (ebook): 978-1-949673-51-7

First Edition
Printed in the United States of America
1   3   5   7   9   10   8   6   4   2

To my favorite Social Security beneficiary, to whom I've been married for 47 years: Becky Margenau

Introduction

My name is Tom Margenau. I worked for the Social Security Administration for 32 years. And since 1997, I have been writing a nationally syndicated newspaper column about Social Security. (You can find my weekly column, "Social Security and You," at www.creators.com.)

So, I have spent almost a half-century answering people's questions about Social Security. Because I have done it for so long, I know people's questions almost before they ask them. And, more importantly, I know how to answer those questions in simple and easy-to-understand language.

Over the years, I have developed a series of 10 fact sheets that explain almost every aspect of the Social Security program. In other words, if you have a question about any part of Social Security, I have not only the answer but also a fact sheet to help you understand all of the aspects of the issue you are interested in. Each fact sheet also answers other questions about the topic you didn't think to ask. And it does all that in a simple and readable way.

And now, I have gathered those fact sheets together in this book.

Before we go on, here is one apology. I hate jargon and internal Social Security Administration acronyms and abbreviations, and I have refrained from using any of them in this book. But there is one exception. And that is the term "full retirement age," or FRA. Life used to be simple. There was only one Social Security retirement age for all Americans, and that was 65. But in the 1980s, Congress raised the retirement age to 67. And they did so in gradual monthly increments over a 50-year period. (See Fact Sheet No. 1 for a chart listing your retirement age.) That is the age at which you can get your full retirement benefits, so it is called the "full retirement age." Throughout this book, I have to use that awkward term, or its abbreviation, FRA, because we all have different full retirement ages. Sorry!

If you still have questions after you've read the appropriate fact sheets in this book, I am willing to help. Just send me an email at thomas.margenau@comcast.net.

Or you can go straight to the source: the Social Security Administration. Call the SSA at 800-772-1213. Or visit the SSA's website at www.socialsecurity.gov.

Contents

Before we get to the fact sheets and learn how Social Security works, let's learn how it doesn't work. In other words, let's clear up some of the many myths and misunderstandings that people have about Social Security.

This fact sheet provides an introduction to the Social Security program. It also includes a very brief overview of Medicare.

Who should read this fact sheet?

Everyone. It provides background information about Social Security, gives a brief overview of its history and serves as a basic guide to the nuts and bolts of the various Social Security programs.

In the first section of this book, I list the top 10 myths about Social Security that have misled people for years. Most of those myths are dispelled throughout all the other fact sheets in this book. But political and financing myths are tackled head-on in this fact sheet. This fact sheet also discusses realistic proposals for Social Security reform.

Who should read this fact sheet?

Anyone who has heard any of the many rumors about how Social Security works and is financed. For example, "Congress has stolen Social Security money and used it for other purposes!" That's a myth. If you want to learn the facts, read this fact sheet. If you couldn't care less about the politics and financing of Social Security, skip it.

Fact Sheet No. 3: When To Take Your Social Security Benefits
Page 28

There is no question I am asked more often than this: "When should I file for my Social Security benefits?" I am not a financial planner. But I am a Social Security expert. So, this fact sheet tells you everything you need to know about the rules and regulations associated with Social Security retirement benefits. Once you read this fact sheet and get a basic understanding of the nuts and bolts of Social Security rules, you should be able to make a better decision about when to start your Social Security benefits. This is, by far, my most popular fact sheet.

Who should read this fact sheet?

Everyone who is starting to think about filing for Social Security benefits. It will explain all the rules to you, answer all your questions and help you make a more informed decision about when to take Social Security.

Fact Sheet No. 4: Working After Retirement and the Earnings Penalty
Page 43

There is probably no Social Security regulation that causes more confusion and consternation for beneficiaries (and, for that matter, more headaches for Social Security Administration employees) than the rule that limits how much someone can earn while getting Social Security benefits. If you are over your full retirement age, the rules are easy. There is no limit. But if you are under your FRA, then watch out — and read this fact sheet!

Who should read this fact sheet?

If you are thinking about signing up for Social Security benefits and you are still working, you should read this fact sheet in conjunction with Fact Sheet No. 3. If you are under your full retirement age and already getting Social Security benefits, and you take a part-time job, you should read just this fact sheet to understand how your earnings might reduce your Social Security benefits.

Fact Sheet No. 5: A Woman's Guide to Social Security

Page 49

This fact sheet primarily covers benefits available to spouses and to widows, including divorced spouses and widows. It was written with women in mind because about 95% of all benefits paid to spouses and widows goes to women. Why is that? Because, traditionally, women have made less money than men. And women tend to take more time off work to raise children. So, a wife usually ends up with a smaller Social Security retirement benefit than her husband will get. And that means she is more likely to qualify for spousal benefits on her husband's account. But all Social Security rules are gender-neutral. So, if you happen to be in a relationship in which the wife makes more money than the husband, the same rules will apply to husbands and widowers benefits.

Who should read this fact sheet?

Both working women and stay-at-home moms will find something of value in this fact sheet. If you have been married more than once, you will also learn the rules that apply to you. And if you are a guy concerned about what benefits your wife (or ex-wife) might be due on your account, then read this fact sheet. Also, any man who makes less money than his wife should read this fact sheet to learn what benefits he might be due as a husband or widower. (As you read the fact sheet, simply switch the genders. Change "wife" to "husband," "widow" to "widower," etc.)

Fact Sheet No. 6: Benefits for Children

Page 59

People usually don't think of children when they think of Social Security, but there are about 6 million kids who get a monthly Social Security check. How come? Either they are the minor children of a retiree or of someone getting Social Security disability benefits, or they are the surviving children of someone who has died. Also, there are millions of disabled kids from poor households who qualify for Supplemental Security Income benefits.

Who should read this fact sheet?

If you are thinking of retiring and have a minor child(ren) at home, you should read this fact sheet to learn how it might be to your advantage to take Social Security benefits as early as possible because of the extra money your kid(s) will get. Also, if you have a grown son or daughter who has been disabled since childhood, you will learn that they can get benefits, too. And parents who are struggling to make ends meet and who have a disabled child at home will learn about the SSI program.

Fact Sheet No. 7: Disability Benefits From Social Security   Page 65

This fact sheet explains how you qualify for Social Security disability benefits and how you should go about filing for such benefits. It includes tips that might help speed up your claim. It has a special section targeted to disabled seniors. And it also explains benefits available to disabled children.

Who should read this fact sheet?

Anyone interested in the possibility of filing for disability benefits. And if you are a parent with a disabled child, even a disabled "adult child," you will find answers to most of your questions in this fact sheet.

Fact Sheet No. 8: Pension Offsets and Social Security   Page 77

About 90% of all jobs in this country are covered by Social Security. In other words, if you work at such a job (or are self-employed), you pay Social Security taxes into the program. But some jobs, primarily some state- and local-government jobs, are not covered by Social Security. For example, in some states, teachers, police officers and firefighters do not pay into Social Security. But they may spend part of their lives working at a job that is covered by Social Security. Or they may be married to someone whose job is covered by Social Security. And there are laws that may reduce any Social Security retirement benefits they earn, or reduce or even eliminate any benefits they may be due on a spouse's Social Security record. This fact sheet explains these offsets and why they exist.

Who should read this fact sheet?

Anyone who has worked at a job that was not covered by Social Security or has a spouse who worked at such a job. Everyone else should skip this fact sheet because these laws do not affect you, and reading this fact sheet might just needlessly confuse you.

Fact Sheet No. 9: When Social Security Says You Owe Them Money
Page 84

For a variety of reasons, people sometimes get Social Security benefits that they are not due — or that they are allegedly not due. This fact sheet helps people understand how to deal with these "overpayments."

Who should read this fact sheet?

If you have received a letter from the Social Security Administration telling you that you have been overpaid and owe them money, you must read this fact sheet to learn how to deal with this problem.

Fact Sheet No. 10: Working After Your Social Security Checks Start: Will Your Additional Income Increase Your Social Security Checks?
Page 87

Many senior citizens continue to work well into their 70s and beyond. And they wonder if the additional earnings added to their Social Security account, and the Social Security taxes they are paying on those earnings, will increase their Social Security check. The answer is, "It depends." To find out what it depends on, read this fact sheet.

Who should read this fact sheet?

Anyone who is getting Social Security benefits and is still working should read this fact sheet to find out if they are due an increase in their monthly Social Security check.

*And Finally ... What To Do When Someone Getting a Social Security Check Dies*Page 91

I will always remember a very poignant email sent to me from a nice lady named Maria, whose husband of 61 years was near death. She wanted to know how to handle her upcoming Social Security matters. Go to the end of this book and you will find my answer to her, with tips for others in similar situations.

Tom Margenau

Top 10 Social Security Myths and Facts

I could write a book called "The Top 100 Social Security Myths," and I probably would only be scratching the surface of all the rumors, misunderstandings, misconceptions, half-truths and outright lies that people have heard about Social Security. Most of these myths are spread — via email, the internet and just idle gossip — from one naive and uninformed person to another.

By the time you finish reading this book, I think we will have cleared up many of the myths and misunderstandings. But before you get into the book, I thought it would help to summarize the top 10 most common myths and, when appropriate, tell you where to go in the book to learn the truth.

Myths about Social Security can be divided into two main categories:
• Political myths (mostly about how Social Security is financed and who gets benefits and who doesn't).
• Practical myths (about how the program works).

Political myths

Myth No. 1: Politicians have stolen Social Security money and used it for other purposes.

This is, by far, the most commonly spread political rumor about Social Security. And it's not true. It grows out of a misunderstanding of how the program is financed. It is such a convoluted and confusing topic that I have devoted an entire fact sheet to setting the record straight. (See Fact Sheet No. 2.)

Myth No. 2: Social Security is going broke and won't be there when young people need it.

I have been working for the Social Security Administration, or writing about the Social Security program, for about 50 years.

And for all those years, people have been telling me that the system is doomed for failure and will go belly up in the near future. Yet the

1

program has been paying benefits, month after month, for 80 years now. How long must Social Security be around before people accept the fact that it is here to stay?

I have always told young people that they should not be asking, "Will Social Security be there for me?" Instead, they should be asking, "How will Social Security change?" The fact is that Social Security has changed often in its 80-year history, and it will change again in the future. But a Social Security system that provides monthly benefits for retirees and for people with disabilities, as well as survivors benefits for the families of workers who have died, will always be with us. And we are not alone. Providing social insurance benefits is something that every civilized country on the planet does for its citizens. To learn more about this topic, and how Social Security will probably change in the future, read Fact Sheet No. 2.

Myth No. 3: Illegal immigrants get Social Security benefits.

Simply put, illegal immigrants do NOT get Social Security benefits. To qualify for benefits, you must work and pay taxes (see Fact Sheet No. 1), and you must prove to the government that you are either a U.S. citizen or that you are a noncitizen living in this country legally. That latter point may surprise some people. There are thousands of noncitizens who get Social Security checks, because they have lived in this country legally, worked and paid Social Security taxes. (By the way, there are also tens of thousands of U.S. citizens who get Social Security benefits from other countries because they lived and worked in those countries.)

But back to the subject of undocumented workers. Several studies have shown that they actually help Social Security's bottom line. How? Many tens of thousands of people living here illegally who have somehow acquired fake Social Security numbers have pumped billions of dollars into the Social Security trust funds over the years and never collected a dime in return.

Myth No. 4: "Deadbeats" on disability are draining the Social Security system.

So many people think the Social Security disability program is rife with fraud and abuse. They think benefits are handed out like candy to anyone who can fake a disability. Actually, just the opposite is true.

2

The Social Security program has some of the strictest rules in the industry about who can qualify for benefits and who can't. To learn more, just read Fact Sheet No. 7.

Myth No. 5: Social Security hands out welfare benefits to people who never paid into the system.
This myth comes from two misconceptions people have. The first is confusing the Supplemental Security Income program with Social Security. SSI is a federal welfare program the Social Security Administration manages for the government. It pays a very small monthly stipend to poor elderly and disabled people. SSI benefits, which may indeed go to people who have never worked and paid taxes, are not funded out of Social Security taxes. They are financed, like all other welfare programs, out of general tax revenues.
The second misconception has to do with Social Security dependents and survivors benefits. There are millions of spouses, widows, widowers and children who are getting Social Security benefits, even though they may have never worked and paid into the system. But they are the legal dependents or survivors of someone who has done just that. Read Fact Sheets Nos. 1, 5 and 6 to learn more.

Program myths

Myth No. 6: My Social Security retirement benefit is based on my last five years of earnings, so if I stop working early, or work part time for a few years before I retire, I am really messing up my Social Security check.
Not true. Don't worry. All Social Security retirement benefits are based on a person's highest 35 years of inflation-adjusted earnings. So, a few years of lower earnings, or even no earnings, just before you retire will have a minimal effect on your future Social Security benefits. Read Fact Sheets Nos. 1 and 3 and you will have a much better understanding of how this works.

Myth No. 7: I am missing out on hundreds of thousands of dollars in Social Security benefits because I don't know all the secrets.
There are dozens of such come-ons polluting the internet that would lead you to believe that if you just knew all the so-called secrets

3

to the program (which they will sell you for a fee), you will come out thousands of dollars ahead in your Social Security investment.

If you pursue these leads, here is the big "secret" you will learn: Wait until you are 70 to collect your Social Security retirement benefits. The theory is that, assuming you live until a ripe old age, you will come out ahead of the game by waiting to get the delayed retirement bonus (between 24% and 32%) that is payable at 70.

But is that really good advice? For some, yes. For others, no. All you have to do is read Fact Sheet No. 2 and you will learn everything you need to know about when to apply for your Social Security benefits.

Myth No. 8: If I am due two benefits (my own and something from my spouse), I get them both.

As a general rule, people who have worked and who are married, or who were married but are now divorced, are potentially due benefits on their own record and on their spouse's (or ex-spouse's) account. BUT you don't get both benefits. You only get the one that pays the higher amount. To learn more about how this works, read Fact Sheet No. 5.

Myth No. 9: If I'm married, I can take reduced benefits on my spouse's record and later switch to higher benefits on my own record.

Nope. You can't do that (unless you are a widow or widower). To learn more, read Fact Sheets Nos. 2 and 5.

Myth No. 10: There is a limit to how much my spouse and I can get from Social Security.

Many people have heard of something called the "family maximum," and they think it limits what a husband and wife can collect from Social Security. But that family maximum rule only applies in cases involving children who might qualify for benefits on your account (see Fact Sheet No. 6.). There is no limit to how much a husband and wife can get in combined benefits from Social Security.

4

Tom Margenau

Fact Sheet No. 1
Social Security Basics

What is Social Security?

I could keep this section very simple and just define Social Security this way: You work; you pay Social Security taxes; and one day, you retire, and you (and possibly your dependents) get retirement benefits. Or you become disabled before reaching retirement age, and you (and possibly your dependents) get disability benefits. Or you die, and your spouse and minor or disabled children get survivors benefits. But, of course, there is more to it than that.

Social insurance

When I am explaining Social Security to people, I sometimes begin by telling people what Social Security is NOT. Social Security is not an investment scheme. Do not try to compare it to your IRAs or other investment vehicles. And it doesn't work like any other public or private pension plan.

As its name implies, Social Security is a social insurance program that was established to achieve social goals for society as a whole, in addition to providing individual workers with support when they retire or become disabled, and providing some support for their eligible survivors after they die.

For example, one of the social goals of Social Security is to raise the standard of living of lower-income workers in retirement. And this is achieved through a benefit formula that is skewed to give poor people a better deal out of the program. A poor person will never get a benefit as high as that paid to a wealthier person. But as a percentage of what they put into the system, poor people get a higher rate of return than their more well-to-do counterparts.

If you need proof that Social Security has achieved the goal of raising the standard of living of lower-income people in retirement, consider this: Before Social Security laws were enacted in 1935, about 60% of senior citizens were living below the poverty level. Today, primarily because of Social Security, that number is less than 10%.

5

A brief history

Almost every country in the world has a social security program in place for its citizens. And many countries had social security systems set up long before the United States got around to passing the Social Security Act in 1935.

That original law provided for retirement benefits — and that was essentially it. But even before the first regularly scheduled Social Security monthly payments were sent out in 1940, Congress amended the law in 1939 to add benefits for dependent wives and minor children of retirees. They also added survivors benefits for widows and minor children of workers who died. Benefits to dependent husbands and widowers were added in 1950.

In 1956, Congress added disability benefits to the mix. And in 1965, the Medicare program was started. The 1965 Social Security amendments also provided benefits for divorced spouses.

This has been a very brief overview of the major changes to Social Security over the years. In fact, Congress passes amendments to the Social Security Act almost every year. Many times, they are relatively minor technical adjustments. Other times, benefit categories are tweaked to ensure people are treated equally and fairly.

The 1983 amendments, which grew out of the proposals suggested by the 1982 National Commission on Social Security Reform, were unique in that they were the first to make major reductions to the program. For example, benefits to widowed mothers and fathers were scaled back. And the retirement age was raised from 65 to 67 — implemented gradually over a 50-year period.

Social Security taxes

Social Security is funded by a dedicated payroll tax. It is currently 6.2%. (It hasn't increased since 1989.) And your employer pays a matching amount into the system. If you are self-employed, you pay the combined rate of 12.4%. Of the 6.2% Social Security tax, 5.015% is funneled into the Old Age and Survivors Insurance Trust Fund, and 1.185% goes toward the Disability Insurance Trust Fund. These OASI and DI percentages are occasionally adjusted to shore up the financing of one fund or the other.

Many people mistakenly think the Social Security payroll tax is 7.65% because they frequently see that as a deduction on their pay stubs. But that includes a Medicare tax of 1.45% that is used to fund the hospital insurance (Part A) Medicare program.

The trust funds

Every day, about $2 billion in Social Security tax collections flow into the U.S. Treasury Department in Washington. That money is immediately converted into treasury bills, and those notes are then deposited into either the Old Age and Survivors Insurance Trust Fund or the Disability Insurance Trust Fund. So, the trust funds do not hold cash. They hold treasury notes. And it is this procedure that leads to all the speculation that Social Security funds have been used for other purposes.

There is a much more detailed discussion of the financing of Social Security and the operation of the trust funds in Fact Sheet No. 2. But for this introductory section, you merely need to know that there are two trust funds, OASI and DI, that hold all of the system's assets.

Earning credits and becoming "insured"

When you work, you earn Social Security credits. Currently, you get one credit for every $1,470 you earn. But no one can earn more than four credits per year. In other words, once you make $5,880, you have earned the maximum number of credits (four) that can be granted to you for the year.

In the past, these credits have been assigned on a calendar-quarter basis. In other words, you had to earn a specified amount of money within a three-month calendar quarter. This led to the term "quarters of coverage." I point that out here because, to this day, some people still refer to these Social Security credits as "quarters."

Insured status

You must be "insured" to be eligible for Social Security benefits or for your dependents and survivors to be eligible for benefits on your account.

Becoming insured is straightforward when it comes to retirement. You need 40 credits (or 10 years of work) to be eligible for Social Security retirement benefits.

The rules get a little more complicated when it comes to disability and survivors benefits. For this basic introductory fact sheet, all you need to know is that a younger person may need fewer credits to be eligible for disability or survivors benefits.

Also, there is a special insured status requirement for disability benefits. The law says you must have some recent work in order to qualify. As a general rule, to get disability benefits, you need to have worked and paid Social Security taxes in five out of the last 10 years. (Once again, younger disabled people need fewer recent work credits.) This recent work rule does not apply to retirement benefits. For example, someone may not be insured for disability benefits (because they have not worked in five out of the last 10 years), but they may still be eligible for retirement benefits (because they have at least 40 credits from some time during their life.)

Kinds of benefits and basic eligibility rules

There are dozens of different versions of Social Security benefits. But they all fall into one of three categories:
• Retirement benefits (including benefits to your legal dependents).
• Disability benefits (including benefits to your legal dependents).
• Survivors benefits to widows, widowers and minor or disabled children.

Retirement benefits

To get retirement benefits, you must be at least 62 years old, and you must be insured. If you wait until your full retirement age, you will get 100% of your benefit. Benefits are reduced roughly one-half of 1% for each month they are started before FRA.

For each month you delay starting your benefits after FRA, you get a delayed retirement credit added to your monthly benefit. That credit is two-thirds of 1%. That comes out to a 32% bonus if your FRA is 66 and if you delay benefits until age 70. The age 70 bonus is smaller if your FRA is greater than 66. For example, if your FRA is 67, you will get an extra 24% when you delay benefits until 70. There are no delayed retirement credits added to benefits after age 70.

If you are under your full retirement age and still working, your benefits will be reduced if you make more than $18,960 per year. (This earnings penalty is explained in more detail in Fact Sheet No. 4.)

8

A note about full retirement age

For the first 50 years of the program, the Social Security full retirement age was 65. But in the 1980s, Congress raised the retirement age to 67. But they did not do so overnight. Beginning with people born in 1938, they started to raise the age in two-month increments. Here is a chart that shows how that worked.

If you were born in:	Then your full retirement age is:
1938	65 and 2 months
1939	65 and 4 months
1940	65 and 6 months
1941	65 and 8 months
1942	65 and 10 months
1943-1954	66
1955	66 and 2 months
1956	66 and 4 months
1957	66 and 6 months
1958	66 and 8 months
1959	66 and 10 months
1960 and later	67

Please note that the FRA for widow(er)s is slightly different. See Fact Sheet No. 5 for more information.

A note about early retirement age

Even though Congress changed the full retirement age, they did not change the early retirement age. It is still 62 for everyone. But there is a reduction for early retirement. For example, if your full retirement age is 66, you will suffer a 25% reduction if you take benefits at 62. If your full retirement age is 67, you will suffer a 30% reduction if you take benefits at 62.

Spouses of retirees

Spouses must be at least 62 years old. A younger spouse can get benefits if he or she is caring for a child under age 16. Older spouses will always be paid their own retirement benefit first. Only after those benefits are paid will the SSA look to your record to see if your spouse can get any additional benefits on your account. The spousal rate is between one-third and one-half of the retiree's full benefit amount. Your spouse cannot get benefits on your record unless you are getting benefits yourself. A working spouse is subject to the same earnings penalty rules that apply to retirees. Those rules are explained in Fact Sheet No. 4.

Divorced spouses
A divorced spouse is due the same benefits and is subject to the same rules as a married spouse, with the following exceptions. The spouse must have been married for at least 10 years. The spouse cannot be currently married to someone else.

Also, a divorced spouse can get benefits on an ex-spouse's record, even if that ex-spouse is not yet getting benefits.

Children of retirees
It isn't often that retirees still have minor children at home. But if they do, those children can get a monthly benefit on the retiree's account that equals 50% of the retiree's full retirement benefit. (Although there is a limit to how much money can be paid on any Social Security account involving children.) Those benefits usually stop when the child reaches age 18. If a retiree has a child (no matter what age) who has been disabled since childhood, that child also can get benefits on the retiree's Social Security record.

Disability benefits
To get Social Security disability benefits, you must be regularly insured. That means 40 credits for most adults over age 31. And you must be "currently insured." That means you must have recent work credits. Most people need to have worked and paid taxes in five out of the last 10 years.

In addition, you must have a physical or mental condition that is so severe that it will keep you from doing any kind of work for at least one year.

A much more thorough explanation of the Social Security disability program is contained in Fact Sheet No. 7.

Spouses and children of disabled people
If someone getting disability benefits has minor children at home,

those children qualify for monthly benefits — usually up to the age of 18. If there are children under age 16 at home, their mother or father might also qualify for spousal benefits, unless they are working, in which case they are subject to the same earnings penalty rules that affect retirees.

Survivors benefits

Monthly benefits are paid to the surviving spouse and children of someone who dies and who was insured.

Older widows and widowers (including divorcees)

A widowed spouse who is full retirement age or older can get a benefit that is generally equal to 100% of the deceased's full benefit rate. Benefits are payable at a reduced rate as early as age 60. The age-60 rate is about 71%. Benefits can be paid as early as age 50 if the widow(er) is disabled.

If you become a widow before reaching your full retirement age, you could employ the "widow's option." That means you could take reduced benefits on one record and then later switch to full benefits on another record. For example, you could take reduced widows benefits at age 60 and then, at full retirement age, switch to 100% of your own Social Security benefit. Or you could wait until 70 and switch to somewhere between 124% and 132% of your own benefit.

Benefits are also payable to unmarried divorced widows and widowers if the marriage lasted at least 10 years.

All these benefits are explained in much more detail in Fact Sheet No. 5.

Children and young parents

If an insured worker dies and has minor children, those children will get benefits equal to 75% of the worker's basic benefit rate. Benefits generally continue until the child reaches age 18.

If the deceased has an adult child who has been disabled since childhood, that child will get benefits (at the 75% rate) indefinitely.

A nonworking parent who is caring for the deceased's child could also qualify for benefits until the youngest child reaches age 16.

There is a "family maximum" that limits the amount of money that can be paid to a family getting survivors benefits. As a general rule, it limits what can be paid to an amount equal to about 175% of the deceased's basic benefit rate.

Lump sum death benefit
The law has always allowed a one-time death benefit to be paid on the account of an insured worker who has died. The benefit rate has been locked at a $255 level for decades. That measly death benefit can only be paid to a surviving spouse or to a minor child.

Supplemental Security Income benefits
Supplemental Security Income, or SSI, is a federal welfare program that pays a small monthly stipend to poor people who are over age 65 or to people of any age (including children) who are disabled.

To qualify for SSI, you must have a low income (generally under about $800 per month) and limited assets (generally under $2,000). The value of your home and your car do not count against the asset limit.

SSI is managed by the Social Security Administration, but it is NOT a Social Security benefit. The money to pay SSI benefits comes out of the general revenues of the government, not out of the Social Security trust funds.

Because SSI is a welfare program, it has very complex rules and regulations. This book is about Social Security benefits, not SSI payments. If you want to know more about SSI, you should call Social Security at 800-772-1213.

A quick word about Medicare
I am a Social Security expert, not a Medicare expert. Although many people usually link Social Security with Medicare, they are two different programs run by two different federal agencies. Social Security is run by the Social Security Administration. But Medicare is managed by the Centers for Medicare & Medicaid Services.

Still, Medicare is linked to Social Security because you generally have to go through the SSA to sign up for Medicare. (The Centers for Medicare & Medicaid Services does not have a network of field offices like the SSA does.) And if you are getting Social Security benefits, your Part B Medicare premium is usually deducted from your monthly Social Security check. There are two main parts to Medicare: A and B.

Part A: hospital insurance

Part A is hospital insurance. It is paid for by the Medicare tax that is deducted from your paycheck while you are working (or that you pay yourself if you are self-employed).

The Medicare age is 65, even if your Social Security full retirement age is higher than that. And once you reach age 65, you should apply for Part A Medicare because it is free. There is no reason not to take it, even if you are still working and not yet taking your Social Security benefits. Those of you with Health Savings Accounts may wonder if you need to take Medicare Part A. The answer is, generally, yes. For more information, just search the internet with the keywords "HSA" and "Medicare," and you will learn a lot more about this issue.

Part B: medical insurance

The other main part of Medicare is Part B, or medical insurance. (It is sometimes referred to as "doctor's insurance.") Part B is not paid for out of the Medicare payroll tax deduction. It is funded by monthly premiums deducted from your Social Security check. For most people, the premium is currently about $150 per month. But wealthier people pay a higher monthly premium.

If you are working and covered by your employer's health insurance, or if your spouse is working and you are covered by his or her insurance, then you probably do not need to take Part B when you turn 65. You can enroll at a later date, after you lose your or your spouse's employer's coverage. There is normally a 10% premium penalty for each year you forgo Part B coverage and later decide you need it. But you do not pay that penalty if you were covered by your or your spouse's employer's health benefits.

Where to go for more help

There is a lot more to Medicare than what I explained here. But, as I said, I am not a Medicare expert. However, I can steer you to someone who is. They are called SHIP counselors. That stands for State Health Insurance Program counselor. To find the SHIP counselor nearest you, go to www.medicare.gov, and pull down the menu for your state under "Find local help," and then click on "SHIP."

Fact Sheet No. 2
Myths and Facts About Social Security Financing
(and Proposals for Reform)

This fact sheet will do three things:
• Cut through all the mudslinging and rationally discuss the politics and policies of Social Security.
• Explain how Social Security is financed, i.e., what happens to your Social Security taxes when that money gets to Washington.
• Give you a chance to fix Social Security by playing a game that lets you pick from a variety of realistic proposals for Social Security reform.

The politics of Social Security

The "third rail." The "sacred cow." These and other phrases have been used to describe the almost mystical standing of Social Security among the pantheon of government programs. No other government program carries the status of Social Security — probably because it conjures up images of everyone's grandma. To mess with Social Security is to mess with Grandma.

But with all due respect to little old ladies everywhere, Grandma needs to be messed with. And if, like me, you were born between 1946 and 1965, you're the reason why. Aging baby boomers simply play havoc with the financing of the system. It's not our fault, of course. It's just that there are so darn many of us. There are currently about 60 million Social Security beneficiaries. And with about 10,000 boomers applying for Social Security every day, by the time all of us cash in our paychecks for pension checks, the numbers will go up dramatically. There are projected to be 83 million people getting Social Security benefits by 2030.

And despite the boomer generation's reputation for free love and uninhibited sex, they never translated their sexual prowess into baby-making proficiency. That means fewer young workers are coming along to finance their boomer parents' retirement. The Social Security system has operated in the black for decades with a 3-to-1 ratio of Social Security taxpayers to Social Security recipients. But by 2030, that taxpayer-to-beneficiary ratio will be 2-to-1. And the bottom line

15

is Social Security as it's currently structured simply cannot work with only two workers supporting each retiree.

Unfortunately, politicians on both sides of the political spectrum have bungled attempts to deal with this issue. Republicans generally promote extreme measures that would throw out the baby with the bath water. A classic example is any plan to privatize the system. (There is a lengthy discussion of privatization plans at the end of this fact sheet.) On the other hand, Democrats try to score political points by putting their heads in the sand and saying: "What problem? Don't mess with our Social Security program."

Later, you will have a chance to "save Social Security." I offer a little game you can play that allows you to pick from a variety of realistic reform options designed to stabilize the Social Security system for generations to come.

But before we fix the system, we have to understand how it works.

How Social Security really works: clearing up myths and misunderstandings

Social Security financing has led to more misunderstandings, more confusion and more political propaganda than has been associated with any other government program — with the possible exception of Medicare.

You've probably heard (and possibly even spread) these rumors:

• "President Johnson moved Social Security money into the general funds to spend it."

• "President Bush spent the Social Security surplus to help finance the war in Iraq!"

• "Social Security money has been used to pay for other government programs."

• "Congress has stolen every nickel of Social Security money and never paid it back!"

• "Social Security's trust funds are stocked with worthless IOUs!"

Here's the real story.

Historical perspective

For the first half-century of its existence, the Social Security system operated on a pay-as-you-go basis. Planners set up the system to take in just enough money each year to pay promised benefits, with a

16

relatively small cushion of reserves (the Social Security trust funds). Every nickel of those reserves has always been invested in treasury bonds. But in the early 1980s, Social Security financing was fundamentally changed.

The Johnson years

But before we get to that fundamental change, let's clear up the myth about President Lyndon B. Johnson.

Poor LBJ. When it comes to Social Security, he gets blamed for something he never did. Our 36th president is often accused of being the first chief executive to tamper with Social Security financing. Well, he did tamper with it. But not in the way conventional wisdom would have you believe.

As one reader of my weekly Social Security column wrote: "Social Security wouldn't need any changes if Congress would just pay back the money that President Johnson stole from the Social Security system back in the 60s." And here is another version of the story as relayed by another reader: "We all know that LBJ cooked the books when it came to the Social Security trust funds. Get that money back and Social Security will be flush with cash!"

For decades now, misinformed critics have charged that Johnson moved Social Security money from its own separate ledgers to the government's general funds in order to spend it. That's not quite right. Here is what really happened.

We all know that the Vietnam War, which LBJ inherited from his predecessor, John F. Kennedy, was rapidly turning into a huge albatross around Johnson's neck. And it wasn't just the loss of thousands of young men's lives that was bothering him. It was also the staggering costs of paying for the increasingly unpopular war in Southeast Asia. He was looking for a way to hide some of those costs, not just from Congress but also from the American people. The government's general coffers were essentially empty. But he noticed that there was an entirely separate government fund that was flush with cash — the Social Security trust fund.

What most people mistakenly think LBJ did was simply tap into those funds and "steal" Social Security money to help pay for the Vietnam War. But that is not what he did.

What he did do was simply change an internal government bookkeeping practice. Up until that period of time, Social Security's income and expenditures had always been kept on a completely separate set of government books. Johnson merely added Social Security's accounts to the general government budget. But this is the important (and almost always overlooked) point: He did not change in any way the method used to invest and spend Social Security money.

In other words, Social Security funds were not touched. By pulling off this bookkeeping maneuver of adding Social Security funds to the government's overall ledgers, LBJ was able to disguise the growing deficit caused primarily by all the spending for the Vietnam War.

Maybe this analogy will help you understand what happened. Fred and Ethel are married. They both work, and they keep separate bank accounts to manage their finances. Fred spends money like there is no tomorrow. His bank balance is always near zero. Ethel saves a lot of her income, so she has a substantial account balance. Fred talks Ethel into combining their assets. Neither person changes their habits. Fred keeps spending just his money, and Ethel saves most of hers. But suddenly, Fred looks like he has more money than he really does because, on paper, his bankrupt account has been combined with Ethel's flush ledgers.

Fred is comparable to Johnson and the overall government budget. Ethel is Social Security. Fred really hasn't done anything wrong. He hasn't taken any of Ethel's money. He's simply using her money to make his bottom line look better.

Like Fred, Johnson moved the balance sheets for Social Security money into the overall government budget for one sneaky reason: to mask his (and Congress') risky spending habits. All the Social Security income made the actual government deficit appear smaller.

This accounting procedure, adding Social Security trust fund accounts into the overall federal bookkeeping ledgers, is known as the "unified budget." And despite its shifty intentions, you could make the argument that the procedure is entirely justified. After all, Social Security money is government money, and it makes sense to add it in with all other government funds.

Still, after the American people figured out what was going on, these bookkeeping shenanigans left a bad taste in the mouths of not only American citizens but also members of Congress. That's why, back in the 1990s, Congress changed the law to remove Social Security funds from the overall federal budget. So, Social Security went back to its original "off-budget" status.

Of course, by doing that, the government deficit, at least on paper, suddenly seemed much worse than it previously did. So, almost ever since then, Congress has, essentially kept two sets of books. One is the official budget with Social Security funds not included. The other is the unified budget with Social Security funds added in.

Having said that, I cannot stress enough that all of this game-playing with the government books has absolutely nothing to do with how Social Security tax money is spent on Social Security benefits and invested in government bonds. Neither Johnson nor any government official since has ever stolen a nickel of Social Security money. But they sure have played around with it!

From the Reagan era forward

Again, historically, Social Security took in only enough revenues to pay current benefits, with a small reserve in the treasury-backed trust funds. But by the late 1970s, that pay-as-you-go plan was in trouble. Because of rising unemployment and out-of-control inflation, the system was scheduled to start running in the red within a few years. In response, President Ronald Reagan established the National Commission on Social Security Reform, headed by Alan Greenspan.

They recommended, and Congress eventually approved, a plan that fundamentally changed the way Social Security works. That plan included a relatively modest increase in the payroll tax and some minor benefit cuts. It also raised the retirement age (over several decades) from 65 to 67. Those changes moved Social Security from a strict pay-as-you-go system to one that would start to build up huge reserves. Currently, for example, Social Security's actuaries report the Social Security trust funds hold almost $3 trillion in reserves! (In fact, the Social Security system is the single largest holder of our nation's debt.)

Should we have stuck with the pay-as-you-go system?

Before we move on, I need to add one side note. Had the aforementioned National Commission on Social Security reform been headed by Sen. Patrick Moynihan (considered the Senate's scholar on Social Security issues) instead of Alan Greenspan, I don't think we ever would have moved away from the pay-as-you-go plan for funding Social Security. Moynihan correctly predicted that Greenspan's funding method would lead to the situation we have today — one in which we essentially owe ourselves trillions of dollars. By sticking with a pay-as-you-go format, we would have had to make intermittent and gradual changes to Social Security over the years to keep the system solvent, and thus spread out the burden of funding benefits for an aging beneficiary base — as opposed to making major changes (as discussed later in this fact sheet) every 30 or 40 years, thus placing more of a burden on future generations.

But the purpose of this fact sheet is to explain the Social Security financial system we have, not the one we might have had. So, let's see how Social Security works.

How Social Security really works

Every day, almost $2 billion in Social Security payroll taxes — coming out of your paycheck, your self-employed neighbor's business tax return, and the paychecks and tax returns of millions of Americans — are funneled into the government. Yes, that's billion with a "b." And yes, that's $2 billion EVERY DAY!

So, what happens to that money? After all, Social Security benefits are paid only three times a month. (Social Security beneficiaries get their checks on either the second, third or fourth Wednesday of each month, depending on their day of birth.)

Despite popular perception, these cash deposits of Social Security taxes do not go directly to Social Security. Instead, the money goes through the U.S. Treasury, where it is immediately converted to special-issue treasury bonds. It is those bonds that are then deposited into the Social Security trust funds.

The actual cash remains in the hands of the government and becomes part of the general funds of the treasury. And it is spent like all government revenues are spent. (If you own any treasury notes, what happens to the money you invested? It's spent, of course.) So, in that respect, Social Security money is used for a variety of government spending: to buy drones for the military to fly over war-torn areas, to help fund the food stamp program, and to pay the salaries of park rangers at Yosemite and Yellowstone National Parks. In other words, Social Security money is initially used to help finance all government programs. And remember, the program has always worked this way — since 1936. It's just that, until relatively recently, the surpluses were so small (remember the pre-1980s pay-as-you-go philosophy) that they were hardly noticed by most Americans.

And some might say Social Security is left "holding the bag." But remember, it's a bag full of U.S. treasury securities. Are they "worthless IOUs," as some people contend? Well, consider this: Three times each month, the commissioner of Social Security goes to the Treasury Secretary, hat in hand, and says, "I need about $20 billion to cover all the Social Security checks I'm going to write this week." (As I said, Social Security benefits are paid on the second, third and fourth Wednesdays of each month.) And the U.S. Treasury has always made good on its promise and funded those benefits. In other words, it has redeemed Social Security's bonds every month for the past 75 years! At the same time, the Social Security system is credited with interest (about $80 billion in 2019, for example). But of course, those interest payments simply show up in the trust funds as more bonds.

Here's the problem: So far, the government has always made good on its obligations to Social Security. But unless changes are made to the system to prepare for the retirement of the boomers (see the next section, "You Can Fix Social Security"), the program will be paying out more in benefits than it collects in taxes. That wasn't projected to happen until later in this decade. But due to the recent downturn in the economy, it's already begun!

Of course, the system still takes in billions of dollars. But more and more bonds now have to be redeemed to cover promised benefits. And if the rest of the government continues to run huge deficits, you can rightfully ask: Where will the government (i.e., we) get the money to make good on all that is owed the Social Security system?

The U.S. government will never renege on its financial obligations. (World financial markets would collapse if this were ever to happen.) In this respect, the Social Security system does not hold "worthless IOUs." But obviously, the money has to come from somewhere. Here's the bottom line: Unless the government simply decides to make major spending cuts to other programs, Social Security will have to be restructured. Payroll taxes will eventually have to be raised, or someone's Social Security benefit will eventually have to be cut, in order to ensure Social Security continues to pay promised benefits to its millions of beneficiaries.

A word about the infamous "lockbox": Politicians and pundits love to kick around the term "lockbox" when it comes to Social Security financing. Most have no idea what it actually means. I'm sure most people assume that the lockbox proposals mean just that: locking Social Security funds in a box. That, of course, would be ridiculous. It would be like the government's version of a person burying his or her entire savings under a mattress!

Obviously, that simplistic view of the lockbox is wrong. In reality, the various lockbox proposals that have been kicked around in Congress would simply provide a legal mechanism for handling Social Security funds during times when the rest of the government is actually running a surplus.

Think of it this way: In any year when the non-Social Security government budget operates with a deficit (in other words, almost every year), Social Security funds are used to help finance other government operations as explained above.

But for only one year in recent memory (the last year of the Clinton administration), the government actually ran a surplus. So, in that year, the government didn't need Social Security money to finance any of its other operations. So, that one year, Social Security money was used to "buy down the debt" by purchasing other government bonds. The lockbox legislative proposals, which never were passed, were simply provisions to formalize this procedure.

Why can't Social Security work like other pension funds?

Many people have suggested that Social Security's trust funds be operated in ways similar to other large pension system trust funds, essentially meaning the assets should be diversified, with a portion of the funds being invested in the private markets. But Social Security finances simply dwarf all other pension funds. We are talking about a program that makes up almost one-fourth of the entire budget of the United States. So, one has to wonder what impact an infusion of hundreds of billions, or even trillions, of dollars in government money would have on private markets. Still others wonder if it would be appropriate for the federal government to be a major shareholder in Microsoft, Philip Morris, Exxon, etc. Other people wonder why Social Security cannot be "fully funded" like many other pension programs. The answer, again, is a matter of size. While all other pension plans have a limited and defined number of potential beneficiaries, Social Security's beneficiary pool essentially includes every man, woman and child in this country — now and into the future. It would be economically impossible to set aside enough reserves to pay all promised benefits to current and future generations of Americans. That's why our Social Security program, just like every other social insurance program in the world, is financed on a pay-as-you-go basis (or, as explained above, a modified pay-as-you-go basis since 1983).

Summary

The principal points made in this fact sheet are:

• Social Security currently takes in billions of dollars every day.

• That money is invested in U.S. treasury securities.

• Billions of dollars in those treasury notes will need to be redeemed to pay promised benefits in the coming years.

• If, at that time, the government continues to run huge deficits, it will be impossible for it to make good on its Social Security promises without raising payroll taxes or cutting future benefits.

• If no changes are made by 2037, the Social Security trust funds are gone, and the system will only be taking in enough money to pay 75% of promised benefits.

Now that you understand how Social Security currently works and what fiscal problems it will face in the next 10 to 20 years, let's give you a chance to fix it!

You can fix Social Security!

When a member of Congress proposes changes to the Social Security system, he or she quickly learns that to discuss Social Security reform is to invite a loss in the next election. So, I suggest that part of the blame for the lack of any action on Social Security reforms lies with all of us. Americans seem to be looking for easy answers. But there simply are no easy ways out of this coming dilemma.

So, here's a chance for you to play Congress and come up with solutions to Social Security's funding problems. Let's see if you can save Social Security.

Listed below are eight commonly mentioned proposals for reforming Social Security (four that cut benefits and four that raise revenues). Next to each is a number expressed as a percentage. The numbers indicate the portion of Social Security's long-range deficit that would be eliminated if the proposal became law. So, if you can find solutions totaling 100% or more, you've saved Social Security!

Cut benefits

Raise the retirement age to 70 by 2063 — a 68% fix
• Good idea: People are living longer, healthier lives.
• Bad idea: Would you really want to work until you're 70? Employers will be faced with higher health care costs for older workers.

Reduce Cost-of-Living Adjustments, or COLAs, paid to Social Security beneficiaries by three-tenths of 1% — a 25% fix
• Good idea: Economists believe the current formula overstates inflation for seniors.
• Bad idea: COLA reductions are cumulative. The longer you live, the more you will suffer financially.

Reduce benefits by 5% for all future retirees — a 35% fix
• Good idea: All retirees should share responsibility for shoring up Social Security.
• Bad idea: Lower-income beneficiaries could not afford the reduction.

Means test: Reduce benefits to people making $100,000+ — a 50% fix
• Good idea: It ensures Social Security is paid only to people who need it the most.
• Bad idea: It would turn Social Security into a welfare program.

24

Raise revenues

Raise Social Security payroll tax by one-half of 1% — a 53% fix
• Good idea: A modest price to pay for long-range Social Security stability.
• Bad idea: The extra tax burden would discourage savings and investment

Tax all earnings (current payroll tax base is $142,800) — a 73% fix
• Good idea: It impacts only higher-income people who can afford it.
• Bad idea: It would be a huge tax burden for the very wealthy.

Tax all Social Security benefits (currently only a portion is taxed) — a 16% fix
• Good idea: All other pensions are taxed.
• Bad idea: It would hit middle-income taxpayers the most.

Require all state/local government workers to pay into Social Security — an 11% fix
• Good idea: All working Americans should pay for Social Security.
• Bad idea: It would jeopardize many well-run government employee pension plans.

What about privatizing Social Security?

When you hear any discussion about "privatizing" Social Security, there are two important points you need to understand. First, you must grasp the difference between "carve-out" and "add-on" plans when you hear politicians touting such proposals. Second, these plans, although they may have merit for other reasons, do NOTHING to solve Social Security's long-range financing problems.

You probably won't find many politicians using the phrase "privatize Social Security" anymore. Ever since the financial collapse in 2008, saying you want to turn Social Security over to Wall Street brokers (i.e., to "privatize" Social Security in the traditional sense of the term) is like saying you want some monkeys with a dart board to make financial decisions about our nation's primary means of supporting older folks in retirement.

But you will hear lots of people talking about using "private accounts" or "managed accounts" to supplement future Social Security benefits. Most of these plans are NOT pegged at current retirees, or even at baby boomers nearing retirement, but at younger workers currently under age 50.

And when you hear talk of such proposals, please remember to ask this question: Is it a carve-out plan or an add-on plan? There is a huge difference.

Both plans require younger workers to contribute money to an IRA-type account that would offer several investment options. The worker could choose a safe but generally low-yielding account or a riskier but potentially more rewarding one. The investments from this account would then be used to augment Social Security retirement benefits.

But the difference lies in the funding details. In a carve-out plan (these are usually the plans touted by Republicans), the worker's IRA investment would be funded with a portion of his or her Social Security payroll tax. For example, currently, 6.2% of a worker's salary is deducted for Social Security taxes. A carve-out plan might specify that 4.2% continue to be used to fund Social Security, while 2% would be funneled into the private account. In other words, this plan gets its funding by carving it out of the current Social Security system.

On the other hand, an add-on plan (usually touted by Democrats) would require a worker to contribute an extra amount to fund the private account investments. So, 6.2% of his or her salary would still be deducted to finance Social Security benefits. But in addition, that worker would be required to chip in an extra percentage point or two of salary to fund the Social Security supplement. So, this plan gets its funding by adding to the current Social Security system.

Each plan has its pluses and minuses. The downside to an add-on plan is that more out-of-paycheck spending would be required from workers to fund their retirement portfolios. But the advantage to the plan is its greater rewards. Most add-on proposals are modeled after the highly successful Thrift Savings Plan, an add-on IRA that has been available to federal government workers for years and has given many of them the kind of financial security in retirement not usually associated with middle-class civil servants.

The upside to carve-out proposals is that no extra financial burden would be placed on young workers to finance the supplemental benefits. But the often-unexplained downside is that huge reductions would be necessary in future Social Security benefits. It's just simple math. If you are going to carve out about one-third of the Social Security payroll tax to fund a worker's private supplement, then, obviously, future Social Security benefits for that same worker are going to have to be cut by at least one-third. The hope is that a well-managed private account will more than make up the difference. Also, carve-out plans come with huge transitional costs. Remember: Social Security is a pay-as-you-go program, meaning the money deducted from today's workers' paychecks is used to fund benefits to current retirees. So, if you cut the amount of money going into the system, you must get funding from other sources to pay promised benefits to current retirees.

But here is the most important point I need to make about proposals for private accounts — whether carve-out or add-on. Although they are often mentioned in the same breath as other proposals to "save Social Security," they do nothing of the sort. Social Security's long-range financing problems are the result of baby boomers quickly turning into senior boomers. For years, Social Security has been working extremely well with a ratio of three workers supporting one retiree. But by the time all the boomers retire (and that will be happening at a quickening pace over the next 15 years), there will be only two workers supporting each retiree. The system simply cannot work as it is currently structured at a 2-to-1 ratio. To keep the system going beyond about 2030, either benefits will have to be cut or taxes will have to be raised. Private accounts do nothing to affect either solution.

27

Fact Sheet No. 3
When To Take Your Social Security Benefits

*Some basic Social Security rules and things you should know
if you want to take benefits before full retirement age ...
plus, ways to increase your Social Security benefits
if you want to wait until FRA or later.*

Introduction

There is no question I am asked more often than this one: "Should I take my Social Security at 62 ... or wait until age 66 or even age 70?" This is almost an impossible question to answer because there are so many potential variables.

And the biggest variable of all is your life expectancy. I could give you a very good answer to that question if you could give me an answer to this question: "Exactly when are you going to die?" And because no one really knows the answer to that question, no one really knows the best time to start his or her Social Security benefits.

Some of the many other variables include your anticipated earnings (if you are under age 66, an earnings penalty can reduce your Social Security benefit payments) and your potential eligibility for benefits on a spouse's Social Security record.

Another variable is children. Sometimes, a retiree has a minor child or children at home. Or perhaps a grown child who is disabled. The fact that those kids could get benefits on your record may tip the balance in favor of filing for benefits sooner rather than later. See Fact Sheet No. 6 for more information.

Yet another big variable is the impact of your Social Security benefits on your income tax liabilities. I am not a tax expert, so this fact sheet will not get into the taxation of Social Security benefits. You will have to talk to a good tax adviser or someone at the Internal Revenue Service about these issues.

Regular readers of my newspaper column know that I tend to encourage people to file for Social Security benefits as soon as possible. That's because I am an "eat, drink and be merry" type of person who wants to spend my retirement income while I am still young enough to enjoy it. I've also encountered too many widows over the years who have watched their husbands insist on delaying filing for Social Security only to die before ever collecting a nickel from the system.

However, any good financial planner would tell you that I am wrong! He or she would strongly recommend that you delay filing for benefits as long as possible, because, statistically, you are going to live long enough beyond age 66 or 70 to recoup the benefits you would lose by not taking early retirement.

At the end of the fact sheet, there are guidelines explaining when and how to file for Social Security benefits.

Basic Social Security concepts

Before we proceed, there are several basic Social Security concepts you need to understand. These are very important concepts, so make sure you understand them thoroughly before proceeding.

Full retirement age

For years, the Social Security full retirement age was set at 65, with early retirement available at age 62. But in the 1980s, Congress changed the law to gradually increase the retirement age over time. The full retirement age is 66 for anyone born between 1943 and 1954. Beginning with people born in 1955, the age goes up in two-month increments until it reaches age 67 for everyone born in 1960 or later. (There is a chart showing the full retirement age for your year of birth in Fact Sheet No. 1.)

Reduced retirement

Congress did not change the early retirement age. It remains at 62 for everyone, no matter what your full retirement age is. Benefits can be started any month between age 62 and 66 or 67. The reduction is approximately one-half of 1% for each month a benefit is taken before full retirement age. (The actual reduction is five-ninths of 1% for the first 36 months of early retirement, and five-twelfths of 1% for any remaining months of early retirement.) For example, someone whose full retirement age is 66 would get a 25% reduction if benefits are taken at 62. If your FRA is 67, the age-62 reduction is 30%.

Note: If you want to start benefits at age 62, the law says you must be 62 for an entire calendar month before you can get your first Social Security check.

Legal twist for people born on the first or second of the month

There is a little-known common law (it's not a Social Security law) that says you legally attain your age on the day before your birthday. So, for example, I was born on June 22. But I technically will reach my next birthday on June 21. That little quirk in the law is usually meaningless for most people. But for people born on the first or second day of the month, it holds a lot of meaning for Social Security purposes.

Example:

Martha was born on July 1, 1955. So, she will reach her full retirement age, which is 66 and 2 months, on Sept. 1, 2021. If she wants her benefits to start at her FRA, she normally would indicate September as her starting month. But because she legally turns 66 and 2 months on Aug. 31, she will actually indicate August as her starting month. So, because of her first-of-the-month birthday, Martha ends up with one extra Social Security check.

This legal twist helps people born on the second day of the month only if you start your benefits at age 62. As I said above, there is a law that says you must be 62 for an entire month before you can get your first Social Security check.

Example:

Ted wants reduced benefits at 62. He will be 62 on Oct. 10. November is the first month he will be 62 for an entire month. So, that is when he will get his first Social Security check. His wife, Alice, also wants benefits at 62. She was born on Oct. 2. Because she legally turns age 62 on Oct. 1, she is age 62 for the whole month of October, so she gets a check for October.

Delayed retirement credits

If you choose to delay your retirement beyond your full retirement age, your benefit is increased by two-thirds of 1% for each month (or 8% per year) between FRA and 70. So, for example, if your FRA is 66 and you start benefits at age 66 and 6 months, you would get a 4% increase. If you start benefits at age 68, you would get a 16% increase. If you start benefits at 70, you would get a 32% increase. Delayed retirement credits, or DRCs, are not paid after age 70. Obviously, if your full retirement age is greater than 66, you will get fewer DRCs if you wait until age 70 to file. For example, if your FRA is 67, you would get a 24% increase at age 70.

And please note that a spouse of a living retiree does not share in these delayed retirement credits, but a widow(er) does. In other words, if a man is getting delayed retirement credits, his wife's rate is a percentage of his full retirement age amount. However, when he dies, the widow's benefit is based on his augmented rate, including the DRCs.

Deemed filing

As a general rule, a claim for one Social Security benefit is deemed to be a claim for any and all Social Security benefits you are due. What this essentially means is that you must always file for your own Social Security benefit first. If you are due any extra benefits from a spouse's Social Security record, those will be paid only after your own benefits are paid. In other words, you CANNOT file for reduced spousal benefits (at 62, for example) and then later switch to full benefits on your own record.

Deemed filing exception one: These rules do NOT apply to widows and widowers. So, for example, a widow would be able to file for reduced widows benefits at 60 or 62 and then, at full retirement age, switch to full benefits on her own record. You can learn more about this in Fact Sheet No. 5.

Deemed filing exception two: If you were 66 before Jan. 2, 2020, you may be able to bypass the deemed filing rules and elect spousal benefits at 66 and save your own until 70. This is explained in more detail in the section called "Limited maximizing strategies for some people" later in this fact sheet.

Retroactivity

As a general rule, no retroactive benefits can be paid prior to your full retirement age. However, benefits will be paid back to your filing date, or "protective filing date." For example, let's say Fred, age 64, called Social Security's 800 number in July to inquire about filing for retirement benefits. After talking to a representative, he said he wanted to think about it. In September, he decided to file after all. He would have the option of starting his benefits in September or taking retroactive benefits beginning in July, his protective filing date.

Benefits filed after full retirement age generally will include the option of six months of retroactive payments, but not before your FRA month. For example, Bonnie turned 66 in January 2019. In December 2019, she decided to file for Social Security. Bonnie will have the option of starting her benefits in December or taking six months in back pay by starting her benefits effective June 2019.

And I must make one more point about this retroactivity business. People over their full retirement age are always asking me if they should take the six months' worth of retroactive benefits. But I always ask them why they simply didn't file for benefits sooner. In other words, if you are 67 in September and are considering filing for Social Security and taking the six-month retroactive benefits, you would, in effect, be electing the month of March as your Social Security start date. If you wanted benefits to start in March, why didn't you simply file in March? Why wait until September, let the government hold onto your benefits for those six months, and then claim the back-pay check? That always puzzles me. Still, if you want to do that, you can.

Benefits paid one month late

All Social Security benefits are paid one month late. In other words, the Social Security check you get in October is the payment for September.

Social Security checks paid on Wednesdays

For decades, all Social Security benefits were paid on the third day of each month. But as the number of Social Security beneficiaries grew, Social Security officials noted that this once-a-month payment schedule was putting a huge workload on their field offices and call centers at the beginning of each month. So, they decided to stagger Social Security payment dates across three Wednesdays throughout the month.

• If you were born on the 1st through 10th of the month, you will get your Social Security check on the second Wednesday of each month.

• If you were born on the 11th through 20th of the month, you will get your Social Security check on the third Wednesday of the month.

• If you were born on the 21st through 31st of the month, you will get your Social Security check on the fourth Wednesday of each month.

Having said that, some people (mostly people who were already getting benefits before the staggered delivery schedule went into effect) still get their benefits delivered on the third day of each month.

Social Security checks are not prorated

This is generally good news on the front end of your Social Security experience but bad news on the back end. For example, let's say Mary was born on Nov. 28, 1954, and wants her benefits to begin at age 66 — or Nov. 28, 2020. She will get a Social Security check for the entire month of November (payable in December), even though she was 66 for only two days of the month.

On the other hand, let's say John dies on Nov. 28, 2020, at age 85. The law says John must be alive the entire month to get a benefit for that month. So, John's wife or family will not be due the proceeds of his November check, payable in December. However, if his wife is eligible for widows benefits, she will get those benefits for the entire month of November, even though she was a widow for only two days of the month.

Social Security retirement benefits: how they are figured

This section will briefly explain how a Social Security retirement benefit is figured. It is based on both your earnings and your age. Your earnings are used to figure your basic full retirement age benefit. It's called your "primary insurance amount," or PIA. (In the introduction to this book, I promised to avoid using Social Security Administration jargon, but I get hundreds of emails from readers asking me about their PIAs, so I guess that term is pretty prevalent on the internet.) And I will explain how that PIA is figured in a minute.

If you wait until you are your full retirement age to file for your Social Security, you will get 100% of your PIA. But if you take benefits early (age 62 is the earliest), your Social Security check is reduced roughly one-half of 1% for each month you start benefits before your full retirement age. That comes out to a 25% reduction if you take benefits at age 62 for those whose FRA is 66. The reduction is slightly more the greater your full retirement age is. For example, it is 30% if your FRA is 67.

Now let me tell you how they figure your full retirement age benefit, or your PIA. The formula is simple in a general sense but very complicated when you get to the nitty-gritty details.

Here is the simple part. A Social Security retirement benefit is a percentage of your average monthly income using your highest 35 years of inflation-adjusted earnings. Note that there are four parts to that formula: 1) a percentage; 2) your average monthly income; 3) an inflation indexing factor; and 4) a 35-year base. We'll work backward to explain how things work.

The 35-year base is the easy part. When you file for retirement benefits, the Social Security Administration will look at your entire earnings history and pull out your highest 35 years. They don't have to be consecutive. If you don't have 35 years of earnings, the SSA must plug in an annual salary of "zero" for every year you did not work, until the 35-year base is reached. And please note that 35 means 35! Despite all the rumors out there, your retirement benefit is NOT based on your highest five years of earnings or your last 10 years of earnings or any other number of years other than 35.

Here is a related issue based on that 35-year rule. As part of the discussion of long-range Social Security reform, you will frequently hear proposals to change the "computation years." The reform I've heard most often is adopting a 38-year base. What they are talking about is basing future Social Security benefits on a retiree's highest 38 years rather than the highest 35. That would lower future benefits because the more base years used, the lower benefits are. Think of it this way: If your retirement computation were based on your highest three years of earnings, for example, that would result in a much higher benefit than one based on 35 years. So, adding even more years to the base would lower benefits further.

But let's get back to the current computation formula. Before they add up those "high 35," they index each year of past earnings for inflation. And this is where the formula starts to get messy. That's because there is a different adjustment factor for each year of earnings, AND each year's adjustment factor is different based on your year of birth.

Here is a quick example. If you were born in 1949 and earned $20,000 in 1980, they would multiply those earnings by an inflation adjustment factor of 3.25, meaning they would actually use $65,000 as your 1980 earnings. But if you were born in 1950 and earned that same $20,000 in 1980, they would use an inflation factor of 3.33, resulting in $66,600, as the 1980 earnings used in your Social Security computation.

You can find a complete breakdown of those inflation adjustment factors for each year of birth (for folks nearing retirement age) at https://www.socialsecurity.gov/pubs/10070.html.

So, the next step in the retirement computation formula is to add up your highest 35 years of inflation-adjusted earnings. Then you divide by 420 — that's the number of months in 35 years — to get your average inflation-adjusted monthly income.

The final step brings us to the "social" part of Social Security. The percentage of your average monthly income that comes back to you in the form of a Social Security benefit depends on your income. In a nutshell, the lower your average wage, the higher percentage rate of return you get. Once again, the actual formula is messy and varies depending on your year of birth. As an example, here is the formula for someone born in 1949. You take the first $749 of average monthly income and multiply it by 90%. You take the next $3,768 of your average monthly income and multiply that by 32%. And you take any remainder and multiply it by 15%.

You can find a complete breakdown of those computation "bend points" at https://www.socialsecurity.gov/pubs/10070.html.

As you can see, the Social Security retirement benefit formula is pretty messy. Of course, you don't have to figure your benefit yourself. Just let the SSA do it for you. Go to https://www.socialsecurity.gov, and click on the "Retirement Estimator" icon on the homepage. It will walk you through the process of finding out what your Social Security benefit will be.

Earnings penalty rules you should know if you are thinking about taking Social Security before your full retirement age

In the beginning of the program, Social Security benefits were paid only to people who had retired. But over the years, Congress has liberalized the rules, allowing people to work and still collect some or all of their Social Security benefits. Today, once you reach your full retirement age, you can work and earn as much money as you want and be eligible for full Social Security benefits. But if you are under FRA, the rules say that one-half of whatever you earn above an income threshold (that usually changes every year) must be withheld from your annual Social Security benefits. That threshold is $18,960 in 2021. A much more liberal rule applies in the year you reach your full retirement age.

Please note that only gross wages or net self-employment income counts toward this threshold. That means any other pensions, savings or investment income you have, as well as accumulated sick and vacation balances paid upon retirement, does NOT count toward the income threshold.

The mechanics of the earnings penalty for people under their full retirement age are quite complex. So much so that they require their own fact sheet. So, if you are under your FRA and working, you must read Fact Sheet No. 4.

Starting your benefits at full retirement age or later
If you are thinking of starting your benefits at your full retirement age or later, then things are a whole lot easier.

Starting your benefits at your full retirement age
If you wait until your full retirement age to file, the earnings penalty rules described in the previous section (and in Fact Sheet No. 4) no longer apply. In other words, beginning with the month you reach FRA, you can get your full Social Security check even if you are still working full time. At FRA, you will get 100% of your Social Security benefit.

Starting your benefits after your full retirement age (delayed retirement bonus)
As explained in the "basic Social Security concepts" section of this fact sheet, you earn a special bonus for each month you delay taking benefits after your full retirement age. The bonus is two-thirds of 1% for each month you wait after FRA to start your Social Security checks. For people whose FRA is 66, that comes out to 8% per year or 32% if you wait until age 70 to file. (No extra bonus payments are

made after age 70.) If your FRA is after age 66, you will end up with a smaller bonus for waiting until 70 (because there are fewer months between your FRA and age 70). For example, someone born in 1960 will end up with a 24% bonus at age 70.

Despite rumors to the contrary, you do not have to wait until age 70 to claim these bonus payments. As described above, the bonus is figured monthly.

Example:

Jack was born in 1951 and was 66 in May 2017. He initially intended to wait until age 70 in May 2021 to file for benefits. But in November 2019, he changed his mind. He has two choices. He could claim benefits beginning in November 2019, or 30 months after his 66th birthday. He would get a 20% bonus (two-thirds of 1% times 30) added to his monthly checks from then on. Or, per the retroactivity rule explained in the "basic concepts" section, he could claim six months' worth of retroactive benefits beginning with May 2019. He would get a 16% bonus (two-thirds of 1% times 24) added to his monthly checks.

Automatic benefit increases for extra earnings

If you continue to work after your benefits start, those extra earnings could increase your monthly Social Security check. They would increase your benefit if your current earnings exceed the lowest (inflation-indexed) year of earnings used in your original Social Security benefit computation.

The Social Security Administration checks the wage records of all working Social Security beneficiaries annually and automatically doles out any increases due. Fact Sheet No. 10 explains all of this in much more detail.

Limited maximizing strategies for some people

You may have heard of so-called maximizing strategies that have been employed by some people, usually married couples of similar ages, when reaching full retirement age. These unintended strategies grew out of some loopholes in a 2000 Social Security law that allowed working retirees over full retirement age to claim benefits (as explained earlier in this fact sheet).

But the 2015 Bipartisan Budget Act eliminated those loopholes — at least for most senior citizens.

One strategy, called "file and suspend," essentially ended on April 30, 2016. So, it will not be explained in this fact sheet. In a nutshell, it allowed someone to file for benefits at age 66 so that a spouse could claim benefits on his or her record. Then the account holder would suspend benefits until age 70 in order to get the delayed retirement credits mentioned previously in this fact sheet while the spouse continued to receive spousal benefits.

I point out this expired rule because the term "file and suspend" has become so prevalent and misused — especially on the internet. Many people who claim they want to "file and suspend" really want to "file and restrict."

File and restrict — or the restricted application rule

PLEASE NOTE THAT THIS STRATEGY CAN ONLY BE EMPLOYED BY PEOPLE WHO WERE 66 OR OLDER BEFORE JAN. 2, 2020.

In the "basic concepts" section of this fact sheet, I explained the deemed filing rules. These rules essentially say that a claim for one Social Security benefit is deemed to be a claim for any and all benefits due. In other words, a person must file for his or her own Social Security first and simultaneously file for any spousal benefits due.

But a loophole in the 2000 Social Security law mentioned at the beginning of this section allowed people 66 or older to forgo the deemed filing rules. So, for example, one member of a married couple could take spousal benefits at age 66 and switch to much higher benefits on his or her own record at age 70.

Example:

Bill was 66 in December 2019 and is due $2,400 per month from Social Security. His wife, Ann, also is 66, and she is due $2,000 per month in her own Social Security. Ann applies for her Social Security benefits. And instead of filing for his own Social Security, Bill applies for husbands benefits on Ann's Social Security record. He would get $1,000 per month in husbands benefits. (The couple would get total benefits of $3,000 per month.) Then, at age 70, Bill would file for his own Social Security. At that point, he'd lose his $1,000 monthly spousal benefit but would begin to receive almost $3,000 per month in Social Security retirement benefits, including "delayed retirement credits" of 8% per year.

And note that the loophole can still be used after the Jan. 2, 2020, date, as long as you turned 66 before then.

Example:

Frank turned 66 in June 2019 but wants to wait until he is 70 to start his own Social Security. His wife, Liz, turns 62 in November 2020. If Liz files for her own Social Security benefits then, Frank can "file and restrict" on her account. He can file for spousal benefits on Liz's record and then, at 70, switch to 132% of his own benefit.

The "start-stop-start" rule

There is another uncommon strategy that was not impacted by the Balanced Budget Act of 2015. It is usually known as the "start-stop-start" rule. It's called that because it would involve starting your benefits early — at age 62, for example — stopping them (sometime after age 66), and then starting them up again later, sometime at or before age 70.

Example:

Veronica's full age-66 Social Security benefit is $1,500. She takes reduced Social Security benefits at age 62, receiving $1,125 per month. When she turns 66, she decides she can get by without her Social Security for a while. So, she suspends her benefits. At age 68, she decides to restart her Social Security. She will get the aforementioned delayed retirement bonus of two-thirds of 1% for each month her benefits were in suspense. So, she will get an extra 16%, or $180, added to her reduced retirement check, giving her a new rate of $1,305 per month.

Veronica would have to "do the math." In other words, she would have to decide if it is worth it to forgo her monthly Social Security checks for two years (she gave up $27,000 in benefits) just to get an extra $180 per month added on to her ongoing rate. It will take her 150 months, or until she almost reaches age 81, to come out ahead using this method. I am not a big fan of this strategy. But many financial planners promote it.

Don't base your Social Security decision on politics

Here is an example of a very common email I get from my readers:

"The political future of Social Security scares me. I'm convinced that Congress will make radical changes to the program. So, I am going to file for benefits now, sooner than I planned to, just so that I get grandfathered into the current system. Do you think that's a good idea?"

My answer: It's a bad idea. Never make a Social Security decision based on what you think Congress might do to the program in the coming years. There is no question that Social Security will be reformed sometime in the not-too-distant future. But as with past reforms, any major changes that are implemented probably will be phased in over a long period of time. They won't happen overnight. For example, in 1983, when Congress raised the retirement age from 65 to 67, they phased it in over a 44-year period.

When and how to file for Social Security retirement benefits

Once you've decided which month you want your Social Security benefits to start, you need to know when and how to apply for those benefits.

When to file

The when part is fairly straightforward. The SSA recommends you file for benefits about three months before your first eligibility month. For example, if you want your benefit start date to be June, you could apply beginning in March. But you could also do so closer to your start date. The SSA processes most retirement claims in a matter of weeks. In other words, you could file for your benefits as late as May, and that will still be plenty of time to process a claim with a June start date. Still, to be on the safe side, make plans to file two to three months ahead of time.

About that start date (IMPORTANT — PLEASE READ THIS)

As mentioned near the beginning of this fact sheet, Social Security checks are paid one month behind. So, the check for June is paid in July.

This rule causes much confusion for retirees because a major part of the Social Security application process is essentially asking you this: "Which month do you want your Social Security benefits to start?" That question is asking what you want your first month of eligibility to be. It is NOT asking you which month you want your first check to be sent to your bank account.

For example, if you are 66 in June, and you want to start your benefits effective with the month you turn 66, your answer to the "when do you want your Social Security benefits to start" question would be, "June." You should NOT answer, "July." Yes, the June check is paid in July. But don't concern yourself with that.

How to file for Social Security

Almost always, I would recommend you file for Social Security benefits online at https://www.socialsecurity.gov. The application process is fairly simple and straightforward. It should take you less than an hour to complete your claim.

However, if you have a claim that is out of the ordinary or involves claiming benefits on two different records, or if you just have questions an online application process can't answer, I recommend you file in person. You can do so by phone or at your local Social Security office. To do either, you need to make an appointment by calling the SSA at 800-772-1213.

I also would recommend filing a claim in person if you and a spouse are applying for benefits at the same time — and especially if you are employing the "file and restrict" maximizing strategy discussed earlier in this fact sheet.

When in doubt, file a claim

I frequently hear from readers of my column that they intended to file for Social Security benefits but that an SSA agent told them they were not eligible for those benefits. Sadly, experience has taught me that sometimes the SSA representative is wrong. (This usually happens in situations involving obscure Social Security laws, such as the "file and restrict" rules discussed earlier in this fact sheet.) That is why I always encourage my readers to insist on filing a claim if they believe they might be eligible for benefits. By doing so, they get a legal decision on their eligibility for those benefits, as opposed to just one bureaucrat's opinion. And legal decisions come with a host of appeal rights. Opinions don't.

Documents needed

As a general rule, you need to show the SSA two sets of documents when you file for retirement benefits. First, you have to prove you are old enough to qualify for benefits. So, you need to show a birth certificate. It must be a "certified copy" of your birth certificate, meaning it must have an official seal on it. In some cases, you may learn the SSA does not need your birth certificate because they already have documentation of your birth in their files from the time you applied for your original Social Security card.

You usually also need to provide proof of your prior-year earnings. For example, if you are filing for benefits in 2021, you will need to show them your 2020 W-2 form. They ask for this record because your Social Security benefit is based on your earnings, and the SSA may not have your most recent earnings posted to your files yet.

Other documents may be needed. For example, if your spouse is applying for benefits on your record, you will need to prove that you are married. So, you will have to show your marriage certificate.

If you change your mind

Whenever you decide to file for Social Security benefits, your decision isn't necessarily carved in stone. You have up to a year to change your mind. If it has been less than 12 months since you filed your claim, and you decide it was a mistake, you can withdraw your application and then file a new claim at a later date. However, if you do withdraw your claim, you will have to repay all benefits you have received.

Tom Margenau

Fact Sheet No. 4
Working After Retirement
and the Earnings Penalty

Perhaps the most complicated provision of Social Security law is the one that sets limits on the outside earnings of a Social Security beneficiary who is under full retirement age. And the complexities of the rules are compounded by the flexibility of people's incomes. People under full retirement age who work are constantly being overpaid or underpaid in Social Security benefits because their income might fluctuate over time. This fact sheet explains the earnings penalty provisions in simple and understandable language.

What is the law?

If you take your Social Security while you are under your full retirement age, but you continue to work and earn more than a prescribed limit that changes every year, your Social Security benefits will be reduced by $1 for every $2 you exceed that limit. The earnings limit is $18,960 in 2021.

Note 1: The earnings limit is for a full calendar year, even though you might have started your Social Security benefits in the middle of a year. The section of this fact sheet labeled "first year of retirement rule" explains this in more detail.

Note 2: A different earnings limit applies to the year you reach your full retirement age. That provision of the law is explained later in this fact sheet.

What counts as "earnings"?

Only gross wages or net income from self-employment count toward the Social Security earnings limit. In other words, the law does NOT count pensions, interest, investment income, income from a rental property, etc.

Accrued vacation and sick leave

Additionally, the rules count only income "earned" in the year in question, which may not necessarily jive with income "paid" in a year. A typical example involves sick or vacation pay. Many retirees are reimbursed for accumulated sick or vacation leave after they retire.

43

This money is almost never counted toward the earnings limits because it was generally earned in prior years.

How the earnings penalty works

The best way to illustrate the earnings penalty provisions is through some examples.

Example one:

Bill is 63 and has been getting $1,500 per month in Social Security benefits since he retired at age 62. In January 2021, he takes a part-time job that will pay him $23,000 per year. That is $4,040 over the $18,960 earnings limit. The Social Security Administration must withhold half of that, or $2,020, from benefits he's due in 2021. So, they will withhold one full monthly Social Security check and $520 from a second Social Security payment to recover the $2,020 in benefits Bill is not due.

But things rarely occur as smoothly as that. SSA employees hate this provision of the law because it is so messy to administer. For one thing, earnings patterns are rarely consistent. This is illustrated in the next example.

Example two:

Using Bill's example above, let's say he originally estimated he would earn $23,000 in 2021, so the SSA withheld $2,020 in benefits accordingly. But then Bill worked some extra hours and earned a little overtime, and by the time the year 2021 was over, he'd actually made $26,000. The SSA then has to go back and further adjust his benefits and, at the same time, ask for an estimate for the coming year and begin to withhold benefits for that year. In other words, in 2022, the SSA might be withholding some benefits because of Bill's excess 2021 earnings while at the same time withholding benefits for his anticipated 2022 earnings. And the problem simply continues to compound itself.

That's why SSA employees do not like this provision of the law. It is a nightmare to administer. People are always being overpaid or underpaid, depending on whether they make more or less money than they originally estimated.

There are two other provisions that muddy the picture even more. That's the bad news. The good news is that both provisions are intended to work in your favor and make it easier for you to get Social Security benefits, despite your work and earnings.

The "first year of retirement" rule

A special rule applies to people in the first year they sign up for Social Security benefits. It especially helps people who start their Social Security benefits later in the year.

That special "first year of retirement" rule essentially says this: No matter how much money you earn in your first year of collecting Social Security, you are guaranteed your Social Security benefit for any month you earn less than a monthly limit. And that monthly limit is always one-twelfth of the yearly limit. So, for example, the 2021 monthly limit is $1,580, because $18,960 divided by 12 equals $1,580.

Example:

Mary is 62 years old. She is going to retire on July 31, 2021. She estimates she will earn about $50,000 working from January through July. That is well above the SSA's $18,960 earnings limit for 2021. So, normally, her benefits would be reduced dramatically.

Note: The earnings limit always applies to a full calendar year, even if you were eligible for Social Security benefits for only part of that year. Mary plans to work part time from August on, earning about $500 per month. In addition, she will have a monthly pension and some income from a 401(k) plan and other investments. The pension and investment income DO NOT count toward the earnings limit. And because her earnings of $500 per month beginning in August are less than the $1,580 monthly limit in her first year of collecting Social Security, she is due full Social Security benefits for August through December, even though her total earnings for 2021 are well above the $18,960 yearly earnings limit. Beginning the following year, she must keep her yearly earnings under the yearly earnings threshold. In other words, this special monthly rule only applies in the first year you start getting Social Security checks.

If you are self-employed

For a self-employed person, a different "first year of retirement" rule applies. That rule looks at the time you devote to your business. In a nutshell, the law says that if your net profit from self-employment (as reported on the Schedule SE of your tax return) exceeds $18,960 per year, you can get a Social Security check for any month you spend less than 45 hours working in your business. (Self-employed people should talk to a Social Security representative about how this rule applies to their situation.)

The reduction factor isn't locked in

There is a rule that could work for you if you take early retirement benefits at a reduced rate but are still working with earnings at a low enough level to permit you to receive at least some of your Social Security benefits between age 62 and your full retirement age.

What this provision does is adjust your original early retirement penalty when you reach FRA so that your ongoing rate reflects a reduction only for those months you actually received a Social Security check between age 62 and your full retirement age.

Example:

Tom, whose full retirement benefit is $2,200 per month and whose age-62 rate is $1,650 ($19,800 annually), has retired from his regular job, but he is working part time making $45,000 per year.

Even though he is working, Tom has the option of taking his Social Security at age 62. His initial reduced retirement rate is $1,650 per month, or $19,800 in Social Security benefits per year. But according to the earnings penalty rules, from that amount, the SSA would have to deduct $13,020 — or one-half of what he earns over the $18,960 Social Security income threshold. So, Tom would only be due $6,780 in Social Security benefits for the year ($19,800 minus $13,020 equals $6,780).

In other words, because of the earnings penalty, Tom would get only three full Social Security checks and one partial check for the year. And let's say he keeps doing that until age 66. (Once he reaches age 66, the earnings penalty goes away, and he would be due all his Social Security checks.) That means Tom would collect 12 full Social Security checks and four partial Social Security checks between ages 62 and 66. And when he reaches age 66, this special reduction factor adjustment rule kicks in, and his ongoing benefit will be refigured. Instead of the initial 48-month early retirement reduction resulting in a 25% penalty, he will have only a 12-month reduction resulting in a roughly 6% penalty.

Finally, let's look at Tom's Social Security options.

Option one: He could wait until age 66 and, at that point, begin receiving $2,200 per month.

Option two: He could take benefits at age 62 with an initial 25% reduction and be due $1,650 per month. But because of the earnings penalty rules explained above, he would get only 12 full Social Security checks and four partial Social Security checks between ages 62 and 66, totaling $20,160 (or $5,040 per year times four years). And at age 66, his monthly benefit would be adjusted to an ongoing rate of about $2,068 per month.

Under option two, Tom would get $20,160 in Social Security benefits he would not get in option one. If he chose option one, he would get an extra $132 per month, but it would take him 152 months, or almost 13 years, to make up that difference if he waited until age 66 to file.

One more point: You do not have to apply for the adjustment. The SSA automatically reviews your claim at age 66 to determine if you are due an increase.

You can tell the math involved in this reduction factor adjustment rule is messy. I felt obliged to explain it to you. But personally, if I were Tom in the example, I wouldn't bother with it. I would simply wait until age 66 to file for benefits.

The earnings penalty in the year you reach your full retirement age

The normal earnings penalty rule says that the SSA must withhold one-half of whatever you earn over $18,960 yearly from your annual Social Security benefits.

But a different rule applies to you in the year you reach your full retirement age. It says that in the months leading up to your FRA, you can earn up to $50,520 with no reduction in your benefits. And even if you exceed that level, only $1 is withheld from benefits for every $3 you go over $50,520.

If you were planning to wait until age 66 to apply for Social Security, it is frequently to your advantage to start those benefits in January of the year you reach age 66.

Example:

Mary will be 66 in July 2021. She plans to continue working

indefinitely. She earns $60,000 per year. Her full retirement age benefit is $2,000 per month.

Option one: Mary can file for Social Security in July. She will get $2,000 from July on, or a total of $12,000, in retirement benefits in 2021.

Option two: Mary can file in January 2021. Her benefit is reduced about 3%, meaning she is due $1,940 per month. The law says she can make up to $50,520 in 2021 in the months leading up to her 66th birthday. Because her earnings from January through June are only $30,000 (one-half of her annual salary — assuming she makes the same amount every month), that is less than the $50,520 threshold. So, for 2021, she would be due $1,940 per month for 12 months, or $23,280.

Although she gets $60 more per month under option one, she would get $11,280 less for the year. It would take her 188 months, or more than 15 years, to make up the difference.

Even if Mary will make more than $50,520 in the first six months of 2021, because only $1 in her Social Security benefits must be withheld for every $3 she earns over $50,520, she will probably still come out ahead by filing in January.

Having said that, the advantages of filing in January diminish with the more money you make, especially if your full retirement age is later in the year. For those folks, it simply makes more sense to wait until your FRA month to file for benefits.

Even if you found that math a little difficult to follow, here is some advice: In the year you reach your full retirement age, at least check with your local Social Security office in January to discuss your options. But one word of caution about that: I have heard from more than a few readers of my column that some local Social Security representatives do not fully understand these rules. If the person you are talking to seems confused, ask to speak to a supervisor.

Tom Margenau

Fact Sheet No. 5
A Woman's Guide to Social Security

Introduction

Why does a woman need a special guide to Social Security? After all, almost all Social Security rules are asexual. For example, retirement benefits are figured the same way for men and women. Spousal benefits are also gender-neutral. In other words, a woman can qualify for benefits as a wife or widow in the same way that a man might qualify for benefits as a husband or widower.

But even though Social Security's rules treat men and women equally, society and history have not treated men and women the same way. Men tend to work for a longer period of time and have more years of earnings on their Social Security records, in part because women bear more of the burden of child rearing and spend more years out of the paid work force. And statistically, men tend to earn more than women, so they have higher earnings on their Social Security records.

Those and other factors are why men usually end up with higher monthly Social Security retirement benefits than women. And because women have lower retirement benefits, they are more likely to qualify for supplemental benefits as a spouse on their husband's or ex-husband's Social Security record. And that is the primary reason for this fact sheet: to help women (and their husbands) understand the rules associated with eligibility for benefits as a wife, a divorced wife, a widow or a divorced widow.

So, this fact sheet is about the benefits you might be able to claim as a spouse on your husband's or ex-husband's Social Security record. However, because Social Security rules are gender-neutral, it's important to note that if you made more money than your husband, then he might be due dependent husband or widowers benefits on your record. The rules are the same. And then he should read this fact sheet, simply changing the genders as he does so.

49

General rules

There are some general rules about Social Security that apply in most situations and that everyone needs to understand. Here are some of them.

Your own Social Security benefit

If you have worked enough to qualify for your own Social Security benefit, you will usually be paid that benefit first. After paying your own benefit, the Social Security Administration will then look to your husband's (or ex-husband's) Social Security record to see if you qualify for any supplemental spousal benefits on that record.

Full retirement age

You must have reached your full retirement age in order to collect full benefits on your own Social Security record or your husband's record. For years, the Social Security full retirement age was set at 65. But in the 1980s, Congress changed the law to gradually increase the retirement age over time. The full retirement age is 66 for anyone born between 1943 and 1954. Beginning with people born in 1955, the age goes up in two-month increments until it reaches age 67 for everyone born in 1960 or later. See Fact Sheet No. 1 to find a chart listing your full retirement age.

Please note: There is a slightly different full retirement age for widows. More about that later in this fact sheet.

No matter what your full retirement age is, you can choose to collect reduced benefits at an earlier age. For your own retirement benefits, or for spousal benefits on your husband's account, the earliest you can start your benefits is age 62. But widows can get benefits as early as age 60 (or 50 if you are disabled).

Most Social Security applications are open-ended

The SSA has a rule that says an application for one Social Security benefit is automatically considered an application for all other Social Security benefits you are due. Here is an example of what that means. You generally cannot apply for benefits as a wife on your husband's Social Security record at age 62 and then later switch to your own benefits at age 66. Your application for wives benefits is automatically

considered an application for your own Social Security benefits —
and vice versa.

But there are two big exceptions to that rule. If you turned 66 before
Jan. 2, 2020, and if you wait until age 66 (or later) to file for Social
Security, then you can restrict your application to one benefit or
another. For example, you could file for wives benefits (or divorced
wives benefits) at 66 and then, at age 70, switch to full benefits on
your own record. And those retirement benefits would come with a
"delayed retirement bonus" of about 32%. In other words, at age 70,
you would start getting about 132% of your own Social Security
benefit.

The other exception applies to widows (or divorced widows). A
widow has the choice of taking reduced benefits on one record and
later switching to full benefits on another record. For example, a
widow could take reduced retirement benefits at age 62 and then, at
age 66, switch to full widows benefits.

Dependency

This is an important eligibility factor for spousal benefits. Simply
put, you do not qualify for wives or widows benefits just because you
are or were married to your husband. Instead, you qualify for those
benefits if you are/were married AND if you are/were financially
dependent on your husband. To keep matters simple, the law just
assumes that if your Social Security benefit is less than your
husband's benefit, then you are financially dependent on him. This
does NOT mean that just because your Social Security rate is less than
your husband's rate, you automatically qualify for benefits on his
record. All it means is that you meet the dependency test — just one
of several entitlement factors.

And the corollary to that dependency assumption is that if you get
a higher Social Security benefit than your husband does, or if you get
a higher non-Social Security retirement pension (like teachers
pensions in some states), then you are not financially dependent on
your husband and you cannot get wives or widows benefits on his
record.

What is meant by "marriage"?

Essentially, the Social Security Administration follows your state's laws when it comes to deciding if you are legally married. Those laws are fairly universal when it comes to a traditional marriage. But states do have different rules when it comes to a common-law marriage. If you are in such a relationship, the SSA will go by your state's rules. In other words, if your state recognizes your common-law relationship as a marriage, then the SSA will recognize it, too.

And as you probably know, in 2015, the Supreme Court ruled that same-sex couples have a constitutional right to marry in all states. So, the SSA recognizes same-sex marriages as legal, and members of such a couple have all the rights to spousal benefits explained in this fact sheet.

Duration of marriage

As a general rule, you must have been married to your husband for at least one year in order to qualify for benefits as a wife on his record. To qualify for widows benefits, the duration-of-marriage rule is only nine months. However, if you are divorced, the marriage must have lasted at least 10 years before you can get divorced wives or divorced widows benefits.

If you have been married more than once

If you have been married to more than one man, you are potentially due benefits on either husband's Social Security record (assuming you meet the eligibility requirements, such as duration of marriage and your age). You won't collect benefits on both records. You will get benefits from the husband on whose record you are due the higher benefit.

And if you are currently married to one man, you cannot collect benefits on another man's Social Security record. The primary exception to this rule applies to widows who remarry after age 60. A woman over age 60 can get married and still be eligible for benefits from a deceased husband's (or ex-husband's) Social Security record.

If your ex remarries, this generally will not impact you. Assuming his second wife is also eligible for benefits on his record, both of you will get whatever benefits you are due. Benefits paid to a current wife do not offset those paid to a divorced wife.

Tom Margenau

Earnings penalty if you are under age 66 and working

If you are under your full retirement age and collecting Social Security benefits, and if you are working, the same earnings penalty rules apply to your spousal benefits as they would to a person getting retirement benefits. These earnings penalty rules can be quite complicated. In a nutshell, the law says that for every $2 you earn above $18,960 per year, $1 must be withheld from your Social Security benefits. In the year you reach your full retirement age, you can earn up to $50,520 with no penalty. For more information about how the earnings penalty works, read Fact Sheet No. 4.

Benefits for wives or ex-wives (i.e., your husband or ex is still alive)

A wife or divorced wife is due up to one-half of her husband's Social Security benefit. You would get that 50% rate if you wait until your full retirement age to claim benefits. But if you take spousal benefits before your FRA, the rate is reduced roughly one-half of 1% for each month. The earliest you can claim a wife's (or divorced wife's) benefit is age 62, at which point you would be due about 33% of your husband's rate.

And as pointed out in the general section, you cannot get your own Social Security benefit AND a full spousal benefit on your husband's or ex-husband's record. You would only get spousal benefits to the extent that they exceed your own benefit.

Note: Your spousal benefit is almost always based on a percentage of your husband's full retirement age rate, even though he might have taken benefits before FRA.

Also note: If your husband delayed his retirement until after his full retirement age, meaning he is getting his full Social Security benefit plus a delayed retirement bonus, your spousal rate is based on his FRA benefit. In other words, you do not share in his delayed retirement bonus. But if he dies, your widow's rate will be based on his delayed retirement bonus amount.

If you are still married to your husband, he must be collecting Social Security benefits before you can claim benefits on his record.

However, if you are divorced, the law says he must simply be old enough to qualify for Social Security (i.e., age 62 or older). Your ex does not have to be actually receiving Social Security benefits.

Some divorced men worry that benefits paid to an ex-wife will reduce their own Social Security benefit. This is NOT true. Benefits paid to an ex-wife do not reduce any other benefits payable on the husband's Social Security account, including any benefits due to the ex-husband's current wife — if he remarried.

Benefits for widows or divorced widows (i.e., your husband or ex is not alive)

A widow or divorced widow is generally eligible for up to 100% of her husband's Social Security benefit. Widows who are full retirement age and older get the full 100% rate. If you start your widows benefits before FRA, they are reduced about one-half of 1% for each month. The earliest you can receive regular widows benefits is at age 60, when you are due a 70% rate.

Note about FRA for widows

The full retirement age for widows is slightly different than the FRA for retirees. For example, the FRA is 66 for retirees born between 1943 and 1954. But the FRA is 66 for widows born between 1945 and 1956. The FRA for widows climbs incrementally after that. For example, it is 66 and 2 months for widows born in 1957. It continues to go up in two-month increments until widows born in 1962 and later must be age 67.

So, please note that if you are a widow who has also worked, you may have one FRA for your retirement benefits and another FRA for your widows benefits.

Your eligibility for widows benefits and the amount of those benefits depend on the age at which you become a widow and on whether or not you are due your own Social Security benefits.

If you are under age 60

There are two situations when a woman under age 60 can collect Social Security widows benefits.

Situation one: Disabled widows who are at least 50 years old can collect benefits on a deceased husband's or ex-husband's Social Security record. But the medical eligibility requirements are very

54

strict, so you must be severely disabled to qualify. A disabled widow gets 70% of her husband's benefit.

Situation two: A widow with one or more minor children in her care can collect "mothers benefits" at any age — as long as the youngest child is 16 or under. (The children generally collect benefits until age 18.) The mothers benefit rate is 75%.

If you are over 60 when your husband (or ex-husband) dies, but you were not yet getting Social Security benefits, and you have worked and have your 40 quarters:

You will have some choices to make. As explained in the general rules section above, a person usually cannot take reduced benefits on one record and later switch to full benefits on another record. But widows are given that option. You could take reduced benefits on one record and later switch to full benefits on the other record. Which option is best for you depends entirely on the money amounts involved, so you will have to go over your choices with your local Social Security representative.

If you are over 60 when your husband or ex-husband dies, and you have never worked (i.e., you don't have your 40 quarters), and you are not currently getting spousal benefits:

You should apply for widows or divorced widows benefits as soon as possible. However, if you have other income and are under your full retirement age, you may want to delay filing for widows benefits until that time to get a higher (unreduced) rate. You should discuss your options with a Social Security representative.

If you are between age 62 and your full retirement age when your husband (or ex-husband) dies, and you were getting your own Social Security benefit, or a combination of your own and a wife's (or divorced wife's) benefit on your husband's record:

Generally, you will start getting widows benefits — assuming they pay a higher rate than your own Social Security after you file an application with the SSA. But you do have options similar to those described above. You need to discuss those options with someone at your local Social Security office.

If you are over 62 when your husband dies, and you were getting only a wife's (or divorced wife's) benefit on your husband's record:
That benefit usually will be automatically converted to a widow's rate effective with the month of death as soon as the SSA learns of your husband's death. As a general rule, your widow's rate will equal the amount he was getting at the time of death. Or it may be slightly higher. For example, if your husband took benefits at age 62, he was getting 75% of his full benefit. But there is a law that says a widow in these circumstances can't get less than 82% of her husband's full benefit rate.

If you are over your full retirement age when your husband (or ex-husband) dies, and you were getting your own Social Security benefit:
You will continue to receive that benefit. If it was less than your husband's rate, your benefit will be supplemented with widows benefits to take your total monthly amount up to your husband's rate as soon as you file a widow's application with the SSA. If your own benefit exceeds your husband's rate, then you are not due any widows benefits.

Notifying the SSA of your husband's death
The Social Security Administration frequently learns of the death of a beneficiary (i.e., someone already getting Social Security benefits) through computer-matching activities with bureaus of vital statistics around the country. But you or a family member should still check with the SSA after your husband dies to make sure they are aware of the death.

If your husband was not getting Social Security before he died, then the computer-matching procedures discussed above usually will not apply. If you're going to be filing a claim for widows benefits, you will have to provide a death certificate as part of the application process.

Benefits for the month of death
If your husband was getting Social Security benefits when he died, he or his estate is not due those benefits for the month of death. In other words, the law says your husband must be alive for an entire month to be due Social Security benefits for that month. This rule is

often offset by the fact that you would be due widows benefits (assuming you meet the eligibility rules) for that entire month, even though you were a widow for only part of the month.

Example:

Frank Smith, age 75, was getting $2,000 per month in Social Security retirement benefits. His 70-year-old wife, Helen, was getting $1,000 in monthly wives benefits on Frank's record. Frank died on Oct. 20. His Social Security check that comes in November (which is the payment for October) must be returned. Assuming he had direct deposit, the bank frequently returns the payment automatically. But Helen is due $2,000 per month in widows benefits effective with October. As soon as the Social Security Administration is notified of the death, they will process the change. The payment she receives in December will probably be for $3,000, which includes her $2,000 widow's benefit for November and the extra $1,000 in benefits she was due for the month of October.

One-time death benefit

Social Security also pays a small one-time death benefit of $255. It can only be paid to a widow who was living with the deceased at the time of death. If your husband was not getting Social Security at the time of death, then you must file an application with the SSA for the benefit. If your husband was getting Social Security when he died, and you were getting spousal benefits on his record and living at the same address, you should automatically receive the $255 death benefit because the SSA's records already show you were living together. In all other situations, an application for the death benefit is probably necessary. Contact the SSA to find out what you need to do.

How to file for benefits and documents needed

It's generally easiest to file for Social Security benefits online at www.socialsecurity.gov. But because of the filing options available to widows explained earlier in this fact sheet, all claims for widows benefits must be done in person — either over the phone or at a local Social Security office. Although, as explained above, sometimes no claim is needed because your conversion from wives to widows benefits will be automatic.

You almost always need to provide a copy of your birth certificate. Other documents you might need depend on the kind of claim you are filing. If you are filing for spousal benefits, you need to show a marriage certificate. If you are filing as a divorced spouse, you need to provide your divorce papers. And, as discussed above, if you are filing for widows benefits, you will need the death certificate for your husband, unless the SSA has already obtained it from other sources.

Talk to a Social Security representative

Because there are so many variables to your potential eligibility for Social Security benefits, and because each person has a unique set of circumstances, there is no way that a simple fact sheet can answer every question or deal with every situation you may have. That's why you need to discuss your particular Social Security case with a Social Security representative. You can visit your local Social Security office, or you can call the SSA's toll-free number: 1-800-772-1213. You also can go to the SSA's website for more information: www.socialsecurity.gov.

Tom Margenau

Fact Sheet No. 6
Benefits for Children

Introduction

One of the jobs I held while working for the Social Security Administration involved making speeches and presentations about Social Security to groups and organizations. And occasionally, high school teachers would ask me to spend a day talking to their history or civics or economics classes about Social Security. When I taught such classes, I always knew my task would be difficult. After all, almost the last thing a teenager is interested in is something as boring as Social Security. But I came up with a novel way of introducing the topic to them.

I would play a little word-association game. I asked them to tell me the first thing that popped into their heads when I said the words "Social Security." Inevitably, hands would go up, and the first responses always were something like "old people." Or some kid might say, "Yeah, my grandparents get Social Security." Other responses were "some kind of government program" or "taxes out of my paycheck."

But then I would say, "How come none of you said children?" I would get blank stares. And then I would tell them this: "When I was sitting where you are sitting, I was getting a Social Security check." And then I'd ask them, "How come?" Most of the kids would have puzzled looks on their faces. But inevitably, one kid would blurt out, "Like, maybe, did your parents die?"

And that was right. My dad died when I was young. And my mother, sister, two brothers and I started getting monthly survivors benefits on his Social Security record. It wasn't much. I think I got all of $22 per month (this was way back in the 1960s). But the point I was trying to make to the kids in that classroom was that Social Security was not just something for old people. People of any age, including children, might find themselves getting a Social Security check long before they ever expected it would happen.

What do we mean by "children"?

A child can be your biological child, or it can be a stepchild. The

59

definition of "child" for Social Security purposes also includes adopted children and children born outside of wedlock. In very rare cases, it also can include grandchildren. More about that later in this fact sheet.

As a general rule, children under the age of 18 might qualify for Social Security benefits, usually on the account of a parent.

Benefits normally stop once the child turns 18, but they can continue until age 19 if the child is still in high school.

There is another large category of "children" getting Social Security benefits on a parent's account. And these are called "disabled adult children." I just said that benefits to children normally stop at 18. But those benefits can continue into adulthood if the child is disabled. In other words, there are many "children" getting Social Security benefits who are in their 30s, 40s and even older because they have been disabled since childhood.

A disabled child might also qualify for Supplemental Security Income benefits. That is explained in more detail later in this fact sheet.

Children of retirees

Although it isn't very common, there are times when a retiree might still have minor children at home. For obvious biological reasons, this would be extremely rare for a retired woman in her 60s. But, of course, it isn't uncommon for an older man to have minor children at home. And more often than not, these will be children or stepchildren from a second marriage to a younger woman.

A child is due an amount equal to 50% of the retiree's full retirement age Social Security benefit, even if he or she took reduced benefits at an earlier age.

An incentive to file for early retirement

As explained in Fact Sheet No. 3, conventional wisdom suggests you wait as long as possible before filing for your retirement benefits. But the extra amount payable to your child or children frequently makes filing for early retirement an attractive option.

But the law sets a limit to how much money can be paid to a family that includes children. It is known as the "family maximum." The rules for determining the family maximum are too complicated to explain in this short fact sheet. The family maximum for a retiree usually ends up being between 150% and 182% of the retiree's full benefit rate.

Example:

John took reduced retirement benefits at age 62. His full retirement rate is $2,000, but he is getting $1,500 per month. He has twin daughters who are 16 years old and a son who is 14. Each child is technically due 50% of John's $2,000 full retirement benefit, or $1,000. So, total benefits payable to John and his children would normally be $4,500. But the family maximum limits the amount payable to the family. For this example, I will say that the maximum in John's case is 175% of his $2,000 full benefit rate. That comes out to $3,500. Of that, John gets his $1,500 retirement check. So, that leaves $2,000 that will be split between the three children.

What about the kids' other parent?

Here is a little twist to the story of children eligible for benefits on a parent's Social Security account. The law says the other parent might also be due parental benefits as long as there is a child under age 16 at home. These benefits are paid infrequently because the other parent is often working and subject to the same earnings penalties that apply to retirees (see Fact Sheet No. 4) or because the family maximum comes into play.

Example:

Let's go back to John in the example above. Let's assume that his 47-year-old wife, Martha, is the mother of those three children. As such, she is technically due what are called "young wives benefits" at the same 50% rate the children are due. She could be added to John's Social Security account. But because of the family maximum rules, the family would still end up with the same $3,500 maximum payment. It would simply be split five ways instead of four. Even if the family maximum didn't come into play, Martha would not be due any benefits if she was working and making much more than the earnings penalty rules allow.

What if you have a disabled adult child?

Mary is 62. All of her children are grown. But one of those kids, Tom, who is 28, has been disabled since birth. Mary was planning to wait until 66 to file for her Social Security benefits. But once she learned that Tom was eligible for benefits on her record, she decided to file at 62 so both she and Tom could collect Social Security checks. Mary's full retirement age benefit is $2,700. At age 62, she will get 75% of that, or $2,025. And she will also get a check for Tom at a 50% rate, or $1,350. So, Mary and Tom will get combined benefits of $3,375.

Children of people who get Social Security disability benefits

Many people think disability benefits are some kind of welfare allowance that was attached to the Social Security program. That is simply not true. To get disability benefits, you must work and pay taxes just like anyone who is eligible for retirement benefits. You should think of disability benefits as just a form of early retirement, or "disability retirement," if you will.

So, just as the children of retirees qualify for monthly benefits as explained above, so do the children of anyone getting Social Security disability benefits.

In fact, the same rules apply as those explained above, with one exception. The family maximum benefit for disability benefits is generally limited to 150% of the disabled person's full benefit rate.

If you want an example of how those benefits work, just refer to the examples above involving John. Simply change "John, a retiree" to "John, a person getting disability benefits." However, as an early retiree, John was getting a reduced retirement benefit of 75%. But a disability benefit always equals a person's full retirement age benefit rate. So, as a disabled person, John would be getting a 100% benefit rate. And because the family maximum for disability benefits is set at the 150% rate, that means John's children (and possibly his wife) would have to split the remaining 50% of benefits due after John gets his 100% rate.

Children of a deceased parent

If you die and either have minor children at home or have an adult child who has been disabled since childhood, they will get monthly survivors benefits on your record.

The rate payable to surviving children is 75% of your full retirement age benefit. And the same family maximum rules that apply to retirees also apply to the children of a deceased worker. In

other words, benefits to the family of the deceased are limited to somewhere between 150% and 182% of his or her full benefit rate.
Example:
Frank dies at the age of 47. He is survived by his 45-year-old wife, Rita, and two children ages 10 and 8. Frank's full benefit rate is $2,400. Each child is due 75% of that rate, or $1,800. And if Rita is not working, she is due mothers benefits at the same 75% rate. That is three people each due $1,800, for a total of $5,400. Let's say the family maximum rate is set at the 175% level. So, the maximum that can be paid to Frank's family is $4,200, which means, in effect, Rita and her two children will be getting $1,400 each.

Now let's add a twist to this scenario. Let's say Frank was married once before to Barbara and that he has a son, Billy, from that marriage. Billy is 16 years old. Barbara has remarried. Even though Barbara has remarried and Billy is now the stepson of her new husband, the law says that Billy is still due survivors benefits on Frank's record — at the 75% rate. So, now we have four survivors who have to split the $4,200 maximum rate. Rita and her two kids will get $3,150. And Barbara will get a monthly survivor's check for Billy for $1,050.

Grandchildren

For a variety of reasons, many senior citizens find themselves caring for one or more of their grandkids. And they usually wonder if those kids can get benefits on Grandma's or Grandpa's Social Security account.

As a general rule, the answer is no. The law says that grandkids can't get benefits from a grandparent's record unless both of the parents are deceased or disabled. And, of course, that doesn't happen very often.

The one exception to that rule is adoption. If a grandparent legally adopts a grandchild, then that child can get benefits from Grandma or Grandpa if certain conditions are met. Contact the Social Security Administration at 800-772-1213 to learn more.

Kids and SSI

Supplemental Security Income is a federal welfare program that pays a small monthly stipend to poor people who are over age 65 or to poor people who are under 65 and disabled. And that latter category includes children. SSI is managed by the Social Security Administration, but it is not a Social Security benefit. And SSI payments are funded out of general government accounts, not out of Social Security trust funds.

To qualify for SSI, the child's parents must have low income and few assets. (Although the values of a home and car don't count against the asset limit.) The income and asset rules are way too complicated to explain in this fact sheet. But if you are having trouble making ends meet, and if you have a disabled child at home, contact the SSA to find out if your child qualifies for SSI.

While the disabled child is under age 18, the income and assets of the parent(s) are used to determine if the child can get SSI. But once the child is 18, he or she is considered an adult, and parental income and assets no longer count. So, there are many times when a disabled child under age 18 can't get SSI because the parents have too much money. But once the disabled child reaches 18, that child might be able to get SSI disability benefits, even if the parents are not poor.

Fact Sheet No. 7
Disability Benefits From Social Security

Introduction

There is probably no more controversial component of Social Security than the disability program. That's primarily because, unlike other parts of Social Security, disabilities can be subjective. Compare disability benefits with other Social Security programs. The rules for qualifying for retirement benefits are pretty cut and dried. Show the Social Security Administration a birth certificate and a couple of other documents proving your eligibility, and your retirement checks will start rolling in. The same is true for Social Security survivors benefits. Provide a death certificate, proof of your relationship to the deceased and your own birth certificate, and you'll soon be getting your monthly benefits.

But qualifying for disability benefits isn't so easy. Instead of simply proving your age or proving your relationship to a deceased family member, you have to prove you meet the legal definition of "disability" for Social Security purposes. And although, as we shall see in this fact sheet, the law defines "disability" in a few short and simple sentences, proving you are legally disabled is not at all a short and simple process.

Here is another way to think of the subjective nature of disability. We've all known fellow workers who might call in sick if they have just a slight case of the sniffles. Yet we also know folks who would show up for work even if they had pneumonia! In other words, one person's disabling condition is another person's minor inconvenience.

Let's look at that from yet another angle. There are some people who claim they can't work and file for disability benefits with a relatively minor ailment such as a bad back or a sore knee. Yet there are other people with very obvious disabilities, such as folks who are blind or paraplegics who use wheelchairs, who work every day and don't think of themselves as "disabled" — so they would never consider applying for disability benefits. To reemphasize the point: What one person considers a disability may be vastly different from what another person considers a disability.

In addition to the subjective nature of disabilities, there is another reason the program is difficult to understand — and, for that matter, to administer. Think of the hundreds of different kinds of disabling conditions: heart trouble, kidney disease, brain damage, cancer, nervous disorders, muscular and skeletal issues, etc. The list goes on and on. How do you decide how badly damaged a heart must be before someone can get disability benefits? How dysfunctional must a kidney be to keep someone from working? How much pain must a person endure to make him or her unemployable and eligible for benefits?

And then there are disabilities that are not necessarily visible to the naked eye. Many people with rather severe mental disorders, for example, may appear normal and healthy to anyone who meets them. But their condition can make them just as unemployable as someone with a severe physical impairment.

The Social Security Administration has established guidelines to help its disability claims evaluators make that decision for each potential condition. Yet no matter how much they try to objectify that process, the decision is still ultimately a subjective one.

Two disability programs

In addition to the problem of defining disability, confusion over the issue is further compounded by the fact that the Social Security Administration runs two separate disability programs that have vastly different criteria for the nonmedical eligibility factors.

Social Security disability

Social Security disability benefits were added to the Social Security program in 1956. A separate funding structure was established to pay for them. A small percentage of the Social Security payroll tax (currently 1.185%) is earmarked to fund the disability program. Those monies are collected and disbursed from the Disability Insurance Trust Fund, which is managed separately from the retirement/survivors fund, known as the Old Age and Survivors Insurance Trust Fund. I make this funding point to disavow the commonly held belief that the number of people getting disability benefits is the primary reason why the retirement program faces long-range funding problems.

In addition to meeting the legal definition of disability, to qualify for Social Security disability benefits, you must have worked and paid Social Security taxes. How much work you need depends on your age at the time you become disabled. Just like the retirement program, most people need 40 Social Security credits to be eligible for disability benefits. Although, younger people, generally those under the age of 30, need fewer credits.

But there is a little twist to this "insured status" requirement. In addition to having the required number of Social Security credits, the law stipulates that some of those credits must be earned in recent years. For most adults, that means you must have worked and paid Social Security taxes in five of the last 10 years. For people under the age of 30, that "current work test" is lessened.

The amount of a Social Security disability benefit depends entirely on a person's prior taxable earnings. Essentially, the more money you've made, the higher your benefit will be. A high monthly disability check today would be in the $3,000 per month range. Average benefits might be around $1,700 per month. And if a disabled person has dependents (such as minor children), those children could qualify for monthly benefits, too.

Supplemental Security Income disability

Many people confuse Social Security disability benefits with Supplemental Security Income, or SSI, disability benefits. They are totally different government programs. SSI, which began in 1973, is a federal welfare benefit payable to the elderly and to disabled people with low incomes and few assets. It is funded by general income tax revenues, not Social Security taxes. Both programs just happen to be run by the same agency: the Social Security Administration.

In addition to meeting the legal definition of "disability," to qualify for SSI, a person must have limited income and assets. The rules are way too complicated to explain in this short fact sheet. But in a nutshell, a person must have assets (not counting a house and a car) of less than $2,000 and must have less than about $800 per month in income. That is a very simplistic description of the eligibility criteria for SSI. To find out if you are eligible, you will need to talk to an SSI specialist at your local Social Security office.

Although the amount of an SSI check can vary from one state to another, generally, the monthly benefit will not climb much above $800. And no benefits are paid to the dependents of SSI recipients.

There is one other aspect that adds to the confusion between the Social Security and SSI disability programs. It doesn't help that the SSA refers to one as SSDI, Social Security disability insurance, and to the other as SSID, Supplemental Security Income Disability!

The definition of "disability"

For both programs, the law defines "disability" this way: In order to qualify for benefits, you must have an impairment that is so severe that it is expected to keep you from doing any kind of work for at least 12 months. Or the condition must be so bad that it is considered terminal. (The definition uses the phrase "substantial gainful activity" instead of the simpler word "work." For more discussion of SGA, see the section on "incentives to work" later in this fact sheet.)

In other words, the inability to work, not just the impairment itself, is the key to qualifying for disability benefits from Social Security. Earlier, I mentioned people in wheelchairs who are still working. If you were to see such a person, you would probably say, "That person is disabled." Yet they would not qualify for Social Security or SSI disability benefits, because they are working. In other words, they are not "disabled" for Social Security purposes.

Throughout the insurance and pension industry, this is known as a very strict definition of disability. Despite all the rumors about "deadbeats" and "fakers" on the Social Security disability dole, the opposite is more often the case: There are lots of people who would be considered "disabled" and eligible for many other government and private disability plans who do not qualify for Social Security or SSI disability payments. (For those who still don't believe me, there is a section near the end of this fact sheet about reporting allegations of disability fraud.)

One final eligibility point: If you are over your full retirement age, you are not eligible for disability benefits. To put that another way, once you reach that age, there would be no difference between a Social Security disability payment and a retirement benefit. There is a section later in this fact sheet with advice for seniors between the ages of 62 and FRA who consider themselves disabled.

Tips on filing for disability benefits

If you have an impairment that keeps you from working, and if you meet the insured status requirement for Social Security disability or the poverty requirement for SSI disability, then you should file for benefits. Doing so requires filling out several forms. You can do it online at www.socialsecurity.gov. But I suggest filing a claim either in person or via the telephone. I think this one-on-one personal contact helps make your case. To put that another way, if the person interviewing you can observe your disability and listen to you describe its impact on your ability to work, this can only help your chances of qualifying for benefits. You can start the personal interview process by calling the SSA at 800-772-1213.

Here are five tips that you should find useful when you are applying for Social Security or SSI disability benefits.

Tip No. 1: One of the first questions on the disability application form essentially asks this: "What is wrong with you, and how does this impairment prevent you from working?" Answer this question as thoroughly as possible. Remember that the inability to work (not just the impairment itself) is the key to qualifying for benefits. You should describe, in as much detail as possible, how your impairment (or impairments — see Tip No. 2) impacts your ability to do your job.

Tip No. 2: List all the physical and mental problems you have, no matter how insignificant they seem. Don't simply mention the condition that you consider your primary disability. It is frequently a combination of disabilities that qualifies someone for benefits.

Tip No. 3: There is a big section of the disability questionnaire that seeks information about your medical sources. Thoroughly list the names, addresses, phone numbers, websites, etc., for all the doctors, hospitals, clinics and other professionals who have treated you. The government needs medical records to help them decide if your condition is severe enough to qualify for benefits. And, of course, they get those records from the people you list on the application form. I can tell you from experience that nothing slows up a disability claim more than the inability to get records from medical sources.

Tip No. 4: Frequently, Social Security needs more information than they can glean from your medical records to help decide if you are disabled. If they set you up for a medical examination with a "Social Security doctor," don't miss that appointment.

Tip No. 5: The Social Security Administration actually contracts with a state agency (it is called the Disability Determination Service, or DDS, in most states) to make disability decisions. Shortly after you file, your claim will be sent to your state DDS. Call the SSA to get the DDS phone number, and then call the DDS to find out the name of the analyst who has been assigned to your case. Make that person your new best friend! This is the person who is going to decide if you are disabled or not, in consultation with others, including a medical professional.

Do you need a lawyer?

You may have heard rumors similar to these. "Everyone who applies for disability benefits is turned down the first time around." Or, "You have to hire a lawyer to have any chance of getting disability benefits." The first rumor is simply wrong. The second rumor has some truth to it — but only at a certain point in the claims process.

About 35% of first-time claims for disability benefits are approved. So, that belies the rumor that all initial claims are automatically denied. And one reason a high number of claims (65%) are turned down the first time is because many people file for disability benefits essentially out of desperation. They are unemployed and in need of funds, but not really disabled. Lots of folks, especially the older they get, have some impairments (back problems, high blood pressure, arthritis, etc.) and are usually working despite their medical limitations. If they become unemployed, they figure it can't hurt to try filing for disability benefits. Many of those claimants make up the 65% first-claim denial rate.

But no matter what your medical condition is and your chances for approval are, do you need a lawyer to get disability benefits? The answer to that question is, "Not right away, but maybe later." I will explain.

You certainly do not need a lawyer when you are filing your first claim for benefits. As explained above, this is simply a matter of completing some forms and then waiting for the government to make a decision. A lawyer generally can't change or speed up that process.

70

And if your claim is denied and you disagree with that decision, the first appeal is usually an internal review (called a reconsideration) of your claim by DDS personnel. In about 15% of these review cases, the DDS and the SSA reverse their initial denial and approve the disability claim. Once again, a lawyer generally won't have much impact on that process.

But if this reconsideration is turned down, the next level of appeal is a hearing before a Social Security judge. And it is at this point where a lawyer can come in handy. In fact, statistics show that a high percentage (about 70%) of hearings in which a claimant is represented by a lawyer are approved. That's the good news. The bad news is that most lawyers will take 25% of whatever back-pay benefits are awarded as their fee.

Senior citizens and Social Security disability

Baby boomers (like me) aren't just getting old; some of us are also getting frail. Our bodies are breaking down at a record pace! I'm probably a pretty good example. After a lifetime of essentially good health (I was once honored by the Social Security Administration for using the fewest sick leave days), in the past few years, I've had to deal with issues as severe as blood clots and as minor as a bum knee. Before I turned 66, I probably could have filed for Social Security disability benefits and had my claim approved. But frankly, I just didn't have the gumption to do so. I'm content with my retirement benefits.

But judging from my inbox, many seniors and near seniors are interested in filing for Social Security disability. Here is what they need to know.

If you are over your full retirement age, forget about it. Once you reach that age, disability benefits are no longer payable. To put that another way, a retirement benefit pays the same rate as a disability benefit for people over their FRA.

If you are under your full retirement age and have never filed for any kind of Social Security, then you are ahead to file for Social Security disability. If you are over 62, the Social Security people will probably suggest you file for retirement and disability benefits at the same time. They can start your retirement payments right away. Then, if your disability claim is eventually approved, they will switch you to the higher disability rate.

But if you are between age 62 and your full retirement age and are already getting Social Security retirement benefits, you may or may not be eligible for disability payments. The closer you are to FRA, the less likely you are to be eligible for such benefits. That's because your disability rate (normally equal to your full retirement age benefit) must be reduced for every month you've already received a Social Security retirement check. And you will eventually reach a point where you simply gain nothing by filing for Social Security disability.

Example:

Sam filed for retirement benefits at age 62. His benefit was reduced roughly one-half of 1% for each month he was under 66. He is getting 75% of his full age-66 retirement rate. At 65, he had a heart attack. If he files for disability benefits, and if his claim is approved, his regular disability rate, again equal to his full age-66 benefit, must be reduced by about one-half of 1% for each month he's received a retirement benefit. At age 65, he's already received 36 retirement checks, so his disability rate must be cut by about 18%. So, instead of a 100% disability rate, he'd get about 82%. Sam would have to decide if it is worth all the hassle of filing for disability just to get bumped up from his current 75% rate to 82%.

When disabled seniors reach retirement age

Many senior citizens who are already getting Social Security disability benefits wonder when they will be able to get "real Social Security." Well, disability benefits are "real" Social Security. They are just as real as retirement benefits. So, you will never be switched from "unreal" Social Security to "real" Social Security.

But if you are getting Social Security disability and reach your full retirement age, you will be automatically converted to the retirement program. The money amount stays the same (because a Social Security disability benefit pays the same rate as an FRA retirement benefit), so the changeover will essentially be transparent to you. What happens is primarily an internal bookkeeping transaction for the SSA. When you reach FRA, your benefits will start being paid out of the Old Age and Survivors Insurance Trust Fund and not out of the Disability Insurance Trust Fund.

Children and disability benefits

Because of the work requirement for Social Security disability benefits outlined at the beginning of this fact sheet, few, if any, children will qualify for Social Security benefits on their own record. But many will qualify on a parent's Social Security account.

If a disabled child has a parent who has died or who is receiving Social Security retirement or disability benefits, that child could get benefits on the parent's Social Security record. Actually, while children are under age 18, they qualify for benefits simply because they are minors. The fact that they may or may not be disabled isn't really an issue.

But once a child turns 18, benefits usually end. However, monthly checks can continue beyond that, and even into his or her adult years, if he or she is disabled. The SSA calls these "disabled adult child" benefits.

If you are a parent of an adult disabled child and are filing for retirement or disability benefits after your son or daughter has turned 18, then he or she will qualify for benefits if you can show that the child has been disabled since before age 22. The same is true if you are filing for benefits on behalf of an adult disabled child whose mother or father has died.

Some disabled children, especially those from lower-income homes, will qualify for SSI disability benefits. Because SSI is a welfare program, the qualifying criteria are quite complicated and extensive. You will simply have to talk to someone at your local Social Security office to find out if your disabled child qualifies for SSI.

How other government programs may affect Social Security disability

With one major exception, most other public and private disability payments usually do not affect your eligibility for or the amount of your Social Security disability check. For example, if you get a Veterans Affairs, or VA, disability check, you can also receive Social Security disability benefits.

But please note that your eligibility for VA benefits does not mean you will automatically qualify for Social Security disability. VA awards degrees of disability payments. For example, you can get a 10% or 20% (or other percentage) VA disability check, whereas there is only one kind of Social Security disability — and that is 100%.

The one major exception to this "no affect" rule is workers' compensation. There is a law that says the combination of your state worker's compensation payment and your federal Social Security disability check cannot exceed 80% of your average monthly income before you became disabled. If the combined payments exceed that amount, one or the other must be reduced. Whether your worker's compensation check or Social Security check is reduced varies from one state to another.

The rules mentioned above apply to the Social Security disability program. Because SSI is a welfare benefit, any income you receive from any source for any reason will usually reduce the amount of your SSI check.

Incentives to work

There are many incentives built into the Social Security and SSI disability programs that allow people to work a little and still maintain their eligibility for benefits. They are far too numerous and complicated to explain in this brief fact sheet. So, if you are getting disability benefits and want to work, you should talk to someone at your local Social Security office about the rules that affect you.

In a nutshell, the rules get back to the basic definition of disability mentioned earlier in this fact sheet. I explained that the law says you must be unable to work in order to qualify for disability. What the law actually says is that you must be unable to "perform substantial gainful activity," or SGA.

So, what is SGA? The dollar threshold changes every year, but currently, the law says that if you are making $1,310 or more per month, you are engaging in "substantial gainful activity." In other words, if you are making more than that, then you simply are not eligible for disability benefits, no matter how severe your impairment might be.

But the converse of that does not always follow. If you are making $1,310 or less per month, you will not automatically qualify for disability. Other factors are considered to determine if you are engaging in SGA.

If you are getting disability benefits and want to try working, the law authorizes you a "trial work period," or a TWP. If you return to work, any month you make more than $940 is considered a TWP month. Once you have worked nine TWP months, your benefits will stop if you are still working and making more than the SGA level mentioned above.

This brief discussion of SGA and TWP just barely scratches the surface of the work incentive provisions. Again, you will have to talk to someone at your local Social Security office to learn more.

Periodic disability reviews

The law says that every Social Security disability claim must be reviewed from time to time to make sure that the person getting monthly checks from the government still meets the legal definition of disability.

How often a claim gets reviewed depends on the severity of the impairment. In cases where the person's medical condition is expected to improve, the rules say the claim must be reexamined every six to 18 months.

In situations where medical improvement is possible but not probable, the claim should be reviewed every three years or so.

And even in cases where medical improvement is not expected, the law still requires that the case be reviewed once every five to seven years.

Reporting fraud

At the beginning of this fact sheet, I talked about the subjective nature of the disability program, e.g., exactly how disabled is too disabled to qualify for benefits? A byproduct of that subjectivity is that conventional wisdom has it that the disability program is rife with fraud. If the emails sent to my column are any indication, I'm always puzzled why so many people simply assume that most folks getting disability benefits are pulling a fast one on the rest of us. They think that these men and women have figured out slick ways to beat the system and scam the government and taxpayers out of money they are not due.

As I pointed out earlier, the opposite is more often the case. There are many people who would qualify for other disability programs who cannot get Social Security or SSI disability benefits. Yet, I can tell you from experience that many people claim to know someone (an uncle, a neighbor, a sister-in-law, etc.) who they believe is getting such benefits fraudulently.

If you know someone you believe is getting Social Security or SSI disability benefits they are not due, turn that person in. Call the Social Security fraud hotline at 800-269-0271. Or go online at www.socialsecurity.gov and click on the "Fraud Prevention and Reporting" link near the bottom of the homepage. Your report can be anonymous.

Fact Sheet No. 8
Pension Offsets and Social Security

*Rules that reduce Social Security benefits to SOME teachers,
government employees and people who collect foreign pensions*

Introduction

The word "some" is key in the heading of this fact sheet. Most teachers and many local, state and federal government employees pay into Social Security just like almost everyone else. In fact, about 70% of all local, state and federal government jobs (including teachers) are covered by Social Security.

But in some states, teachers and government employees, including many police officers and firefighters, do not pay Social Security taxes. If you will get a pension from a job where your employer does not withhold Social Security taxes or have worked in another country and will collect a pension from that country, but you have paid enough Social Security taxes in other jobs to qualify for a Social Security retirement benefit (i.e., you have your 40 quarters), that benefit likely will be reduced because of your government pension. The law requiring this reduction is called the Windfall Elimination Provision, or WEP.

The same government or teacher's pension will offset, and usually eliminate, any Social Security benefits you might be due on a spouse's Social Security record. The law requiring this is called the Government Pension Offset, or GPO. This fact sheet explains both laws. (Although, in most cases, someone collecting a pension from a foreign government will not be affected by GPO.)

Note: Some state and local pension systems have unique rules that can affect how their employees are affected by WEP and GPO in specialized circumstances. This fact sheet can only explain how the federal law works. You will need to contact your pension administrator to find out if they have any special rules that could impact you.

Windfall Elimination Provision

Note: This section explains how your own Social Security benefit might be reduced.

This provision reduces your Social Security benefit — generally by about one-half. In other words, if the estimate you get from the Social Security Administration says you are due $400 per month in a retirement pension when you reach Social Security's full retirement age, you can more likely expect to get about $200.

The key to understanding this provision is to realize that the word "social" in Social Security means something. Unlike private and other public sector pension plans, there are social goals built into the Social Security program. One of those goals is to raise the standard of living of lower-income workers in retirement. This is accomplished through a benefit formula that is designed to give lower-paid workers a better deal than their more highly paid counterparts. Very low-paid workers could get a Social Security retirement benefit that represents up to 90% of their earnings. This percentage is known as a "replacement rate." In other words, the Social Security benefits paid to low-income workers are intended to replace 90% of their preretirement earnings. People with average incomes (the middle class) generally get a 40% replacement rate. Higher-income people get a rate around 30%.

The problem is that government employees and others who spend the bulk of their working lives not paying into Social Security are automatically treated as low-income people by the Social Security Administration's computers. That's because there are "zeros" on their Social Security earnings record for every year they spent in their non-Social Security job. The SSA's records won't show they were actually working at the other job and earning another pension. Instead, their Social Security earnings record simply shows gaps in their work history. So, when figuring their Social Security retirement benefit, the SSA's computers automatically use the formula intended to compensate a lower-income person.

But government employees generally can be classified as people with average incomes, so they should get the same Social Security replacement rate paid to all middle-class workers. That's why a modified formula is used to refigure their benefits and give them the proper — and fair — replacement rate. If you're a teacher or government employee impacted by this law, that modified formula takes you from the 90% (poor person's) replacement rate to the 40% (middle-class person's) replacement rate, thus reducing benefits by about 50%.

As a retired federal government employee who spent his career paying into the civil service retirement system and not into Social Security, and who also worked at some jobs covered by Social Security both before and after my government career, I am affected by WEP. But I understand that I was a middle-class worker all my life. I was never rich, but I certainly wasn't poor. So, I should not get a Social Security benefit rate intended for lower-income people. I am perfectly content having my Social Security retirement benefit adjusted to reflect my middle class status.

For those of you who were lower-income government employees, there is a guarantee. It says that if you get a low government or teacher's pension, the reduction in your Social Security benefit cannot be more than one-half of that pension.

Note: To find out how your Social Security benefit will be affected by WEP, you can use the WEP calculator at the SSA's website at www.socialsecurity.gov, or you can call them at 800-772-1213.

An exception to WEP — if you have more than 20 years of "substantial" Social Security earnings

If you have 30 or more years of substantial Social Security earnings, the windfall provision won't apply and your benefit will not be reduced. A chart on the next page gives a year-by-year breakdown of what the government considers substantial earnings.

If you have between 20 and 29 years of substantial earnings, your Social Security benefit will be only partially reduced. Instead of being cut in half, it will be reduced anywhere from about 5% to 45%, depending on the number of years of substantial earnings on your record. The more years of earnings, the less the reduction will be. Call the SSA at 1-800-772-1213 to learn the reduction that applies to you.

There are other exceptions that apply to railroad workers, some employees of nonprofit organizations and people who worked in non-Social Security jobs before 1957. For a complete list of exceptions, go to the Social Security website.

Here is what the law considers "substantial earnings" for each year.

1937-1954	$900	1993	$10,725
1955-1958	$1,050	1994	$11,250
1959-1965	$1,200	1995	$11,325
1966-1967	$1,650	1996	$11,625
1968-1971	$1,950	1997	$12,150
1972	$2,250	1998	$12,675
1973	$2,700	1999	$13,425
1974	$3,300	2000	$14,175
1975	$3,525	2001	$14,925
1976	$3,825	2002	$15,750
1977	$4,125	2003	$16,125
1978	$4,425	2004	$16,275
1979	$4,725	2005	$16,725
1980	$5,100	2006	$17,475
1981	$5,550	2007	$18,150
1982	$6,075	2008	$18,975
1983	$6,675	2009-11	$19,800
1984	$7,050	2012	$20,475
1985	$7,425	2013	$21,075
1986	$7,875	2014	$21,750
1987	$8,175	2015-16	$22,060
1988	$8,400	2017	$23,625
1989	$8,925	2018	$23,850
1990	$9,525	2019	$24,675
1991	$9,900	2020	$24,675
1992	$10,350	2021	$25,575

Government Pension Offset

Note: This section explains how your government pension may offset any benefits you are due on a spouse's Social Security record.

If you will get a pension from a job not covered by Social Security, that pension will offset any benefits you might be due on your spouse's Social Security record. The SSA must deduct an amount equal to two-thirds of your government pension from any wives, husbands, widows or widowers benefits you might be due from Social Security. Because government pensions are often substantially higher than spousal benefits paid under Social Security, this rule generally means you will not qualify for any benefits on your spouse's Social Security record.

Note: This offset affects only the spouse's benefit YOU might be due on your husband or wife's Social Security record. It does NOT impact his or her benefit. In other words, even though you are due a teacher's pension or government pension, your spouse will get his or her full Social Security retirement benefit. It is your potential spousal benefit on your husband or wife's Social Security record that is affected by the Government Pension Offset.

Why the offset?

Benefits that Social Security pays to wives, husbands, widows and widowers are "dependents" benefits. These benefits were established in the 1930s to compensate spouses who stayed home to raise a family and who were financially dependent on the working spouse. But as more and more couples both worked, they each earned their own Social Security retirement benefits. The law has always required the SSA to offset a Social Security retirement benefit against any dependents benefits. In other words, if a woman worked and earned her own $1,800 monthly Social Security retirement benefit but she was also due a $1,500 wife's benefit on her husband's Social Security record, the SSA could not pay that wife's benefit, because her own Social Security benefit offsets it. But if that same woman was a government employee who did not pay into Social Security and who earned an $1,800 government or teacher's pension, there was no offset, and the SSA was required to pay her a full wife's benefit in addition to her government pension.

The Government Pension Offset rule exists simply to ensure that everyone is treated fairly.

Exceptions

This rule affects most government workers who do not pay into Social Security. But there are some exceptions that apply in very rare situations. For a list of those exceptions, go to www.socialsecurity.gov/pubs/10007.html. Also, GPO usually will not affect you if you collect a pension from another country.

An example that explains the fairness of the government pension offset:

Many teachers and government employees affected by the government pension offset think the law is unfair. They believe they are being cheated out of Social Security benefits that everyone else gets.

But let's meet Bob and Carol — and their neighbors Ted and Alice. They live in a nice suburb of Dallas. Their stories explain why the pension offset is fair.

Bob and Carol both worked all their lives. And they worked at jobs that were covered by Social Security. In other words, Social Security taxes were deducted from both their paychecks.

Neighbor Ted also worked at a job covered by Social Security. But his wife, Alice, was a teacher in Dallas. Texas teachers pay into the Texas Teacher's Retirement System, but they do not pay into Social Security.

Bob retired and is getting $1,200 per month in Social Security retirement benefits. Carol actually made a little more than Bob most of her life, so she's getting a Social Security retirement pension of about $1,500 per month. Carol can't get (and, frankly, doesn't expect) any wives benefits on Bob's record, because her own Social Security benefit precludes any spousal payments. In other words, Carol's own retirement benefit offsets any wives benefits she might have been due on her husband's record. And for that matter, Bob can't get a husband's benefit on Carol's record, because his own retirement benefit would offset it.

Across the street, Ted is getting roughly the same Social Security benefit as Bob, about $1,200 per month. Alice is getting a $3,000 monthly teacher's pension. Before the pension offset law was in place, Alice would have received a $600 dependent wife's benefit from Social Security in addition to her teacher's pension. Alice is mysteriously upset because she can't get a wife's benefit on Ted's Social Security record. The Government Pension Offset law prevents that from happening. Alice thinks she and other teachers are being singled out for Social Security penalties. What she doesn't understand is the law treats her the same way her neighbor Carol is being treated. Again, it says that neither woman will get a dependent wife's benefit from Social Security, because they're getting their own retirement pensions.

An important Medicare message
Even though you may not qualify for monthly cash benefits on your spouse's Social Security record, you still can get Medicare on that spouse's record if you are 65 or older and if you can't get Medicare on your own record.

Fact Sheet No. 9
When Social Security Says
You Owe Them Money

Introduction

If you get a letter from the Social Security Administration telling you that you received more benefits than you were due and demanding repayment, don't panic. Instead, read the letter carefully, and consider your options. Also, read this fact sheet, which will help you understand how to deal with this disturbing situation.

There are many different reasons why people may have received benefits they are not due. The most common scenario involves the confusing earnings penalty rules. These are the rules that limit the amount of money a Social Security beneficiary under their full retirement age can make. (These rules are explained in Fact Sheet No. 4.)

Other folks get overpaid because they failed to report something that could affect their eligibility for Social Security benefits, such as the receipt of a pension from a job that was not covered by Social Security. In very rare cases, a person can get overpaid because the SSA simply miscalculated his or her benefit.

What you do about the overpayment depends on whether or not you accept the SSA's allegation that you have been overpaid.

If you agree with the overpayment decision

If you acknowledge the fact that you received benefits you are not due, there are several ways you can repay the overpayment.

If you are still getting monthly Social Security benefits, the overpayment letter usually says the SSA will withhold your full monthly checks until the overpaid amount has been recovered. If you are OK with that, there is nothing you need to do.

If you do not want to or cannot afford to have your full monthly benefits withheld, you can ask that the overpayment be held back in monthly installments. SSA rules say they must try to recover the overpayment within a 36-month period. However, if that would be a hardship for you, you can try to negotiate with them to pay back the overpaid funds over a longer period of time.

If you are no longer getting Social Security benefits when you receive an overpayment letter, you can simply write a check for the amount of the overpayment payable to the Social Security Administration. Or you can work with the SSA to repay the amount in monthly installments as explained above.

If you don't understand or you disagree with the overpayment decision

If you do not agree that you are overpaid, or you simply are confused about the alleged overpayment, then you need to take further action. In most cases, the overpayment letter will tell you that you have 60 days to take one of the following actions.

You should start out by calling the SSA at 800-772-1213. You could just discuss the overpayment with someone over the phone. But you might want to make an appointment to talk to someone in person at your local Social Security office.

If you are not satisfied with the explanation or still do not understand the reason for the overpayment, you should file a formal appeal of the overpayment. You will probably be asked to fill out a "Request for Reconsideration" form. On that form, you will indicate why you disagree with the overpayment decision.

By filing the reconsideration request, your claim will be reviewed by someone within the SSA who was not involved in the first decision that you were overpaid. And this will eventually result in a second letter to you containing another decision about your overpayment. If it is a favorable decision (meaning you are not overpaid), then your case is essentially closed.

But if the reconsidered opinion upholds their initial allegation that you are overpaid, you must either accept their decision and make arrangements to repay the overpayment (see above), file a second appeal or consider an overpayment waiver request.

Filing a second appeal may eventually lead to a higher-level review of your case, including a possible hearing in which you will be invited to give evidence about why you think you are not overpaid.

If, following the hearing, you are still considered overpaid, you must either accept their decision and make arrangements to repay the overpayment (see above) or consider an overpayment waiver request (see below).

Waiver of an overpayment

The SSA will waive an overpayment, meaning they will simply write it off, if both of the following conditions are met:

No. 1: You cannot afford to repay the overpayment.

No. 2: It was not your fault that the overpayment occurred.

To file for a waiver, contact the SSA at 800-772-1213, and tell them you want to complete the waiver request form. You usually have 60 days from the date of the overpayment letter to fill out the waiver form.

I cannot stress enough how important it is that you meet both conditions for a waiver. Many people claim they cannot afford to repay the overpayment. However, no matter how dire your financial circumstances are, if the overpayment was your fault, then you will be required to repay it.

To determine if you are financially unable to repay the overpayment, the waiver request form asks you to list your monthly income and your monthly expenses. If your income exceeds your expenses, there is a good chance your waiver request will be denied.

To determine if you are without fault, the waiver request form asks you to explain why you believe it was not your fault that you were overpaid in the first place. The SSA can be quite strict when evaluating your without-fault allegation. For example, if you were overpaid because your earnings exceeded the income threshold limits, and you claim that you reported your earnings to the agency but they failed to reduce your benefits, they could then say that you should have known that you were not due the benefits that they mistakenly sent and therefore should have returned the excess benefits. In other words, even though the SSA failed to take action on your report, they could still claim that the overpayment was your fault because you accepted benefits you knew you were not due.

If your waiver request is approved, the overpayment simply goes away. If your waiver request is denied, you can file an appeal of that decision, if you want. Or you can simply accept the fact that you got money from the SSA that you were not due and make arrangements to repay it.

Fact Sheet No. 10
Working After Your Social Security Checks Start: Will Your Additional Income Increase the Amount of Your Social Security Check?

Three Questions

People who continue to work after going on Social Security usually have three questions concerning their work and its impact on their Social Security benefits.

Question one

How much money can I make before my Social Security benefits are reduced?

Answer: If you are over your full retirement age, your income has no effect on your Social Security checks. But it's a different story if you are under your FRA. The Social Security earnings penalty rules are quite complicated. To learn more about them, see Fact Sheet No. 4.

Question two

If I work, do I have to pay Social Security taxes even though I am already receiving Social Security benefits?

Answer: Yes. Everyone who works (at a job covered by Social Security) must have Social Security payroll taxes deducted from his or her paycheck. If you run your own business, you must pay Social Security self-employment taxes when you file your annual tax return. And you pay those taxes (payroll or self-employment) whether you are 10 years old or 110 years old!

Question three

Will those extra taxes I pay increase the amount of my Social Security check?

Answer: The answer to this question is, "It depends!" And explaining that wishy-washy answer is the primary reason for this fact sheet.

How Social Security benefits are figured

To understand whether or not the earnings you have and the taxes you pay will increase your benefits after you start getting Social Security, you have to understand how Social Security retirement benefits are figured in the first place.

Simply stated, your Social Security retirement benefit is based on your average monthly income, indexed for inflation, using a 35-year base of earnings. So, when you initially filed for Social Security, the Social Security Administration looked at your entire earnings history. Then they adjusted each year of earnings for inflation. The inflation adjustment factor depends on your year of birth and varies from one year to the next.

Here is just one example. Let's say Mike was born in 1949. And let's say that he made $7,000 in 1970. When figuring his Social Security benefit, the SSA multiplied that $7,000 by an inflation adjustment factor of 6.58. In other words, instead of $7,000, they actually used $46,060 as his 1970 earnings when figuring his Social Security benefit.

Because there are literally thousands of these inflation factors — depending on your date of birth and the year in question — I simply cannot list them here. The SSA produces a pamphlet for each year of birth (for recent retirees) that lists these inflation factors. If you're interested, go to www.socialsecurity.gov/pubs and click on "Retirement." Then find the publication labeled "Your Retirement Benefit: How It Is Figured" for your year of birth and click on it.

And now, back to our retirement calculation. After the SSA indexes each year of earnings for inflation, they pull out your highest 35 years and add them up. Then they divide the total by 420 — that's the number of months in 35 years — to get your average monthly inflation-adjusted income. Your Social Security benefit is a percentage of that amount. The percentage used depends on a variety of factors (explained in the publication referred to in the prior paragraph). But for the purposes of this fact sheet, we don't need to know the precise percentage. Suffice it to say that for most people, their Social Security retirement benefit represents roughly 40% of their average inflation-adjusted monthly income.

The big IF!
So, when you are working and paying Social Security taxes after you start receiving Social Security benefits, those additional taxes you are paying will increase your monthly Social Security check IF your current earnings increase your average monthly income. In other words, IF your current annual income is higher than the lowest inflation-adjusted year of earnings used in your most recent Social Security computation, the SSA will drop out that low year, add in the new higher year, recalculate your average monthly income and then refigure your Social Security benefit.

Example:

Let's go back to Mike's case cited above. Let's say that the $7,000 he made in 1970 was the lowest year in his current Social Security computation. And let's further say that he is still working and made $35,000 last year. Mike assumes that because $35,000 is much higher than $7,000, he should get an increase in his Social Security checks. But remember, the SSA didn't use $7,000 in his benefit calculation. They used the inflation-adjusted amount of $46,060. Because his current earnings of $35,000 are lower than the low year of $46,060 used in his Social Security retirement computation, the additional earnings do NOT increase his average monthly income, so his Social Security benefit will not be increased.

On the other hand, had Mike made $70,000, for example, that would increase his benefit. The SSA would replace this current low year of $46,060 with the new higher year of $70,000, recompute his average monthly wage and refigure his benefit.

How much will he get? It depends entirely on Mike's past earnings and his current income. Monthly benefit increases can be as little as $5 or upward of $50. But on average, a year of earnings will increase your Social Security benefit by about $20 per month.

The increase comes automatically
The SSA has a software program that automatically tracks the earnings of working Social Security beneficiaries and refigures their benefits to see if any increase is due. It's called the Automated Earnings Reappraisal Operation, or AERO. It generally happens between May and October of each year.

In other words, IF you are getting Social Security benefits, and IF you are working, and IF your latest earnings increase your average monthly wage and thus your Social Security benefit, you generally will see that increase by October of the following year. For example, you would get an increase for your 2020 earnings by October 2021. The SSA sends you a notice indicating the increase in your monthly benefit, which is retroactive to January of the year you get the notice.

If you don't get an increase, that probably means your earnings were simply not high enough to raise your average monthly income and thus your Social Security benefit. The SSA has a very high percentage of accuracy when computing these increases. However, if you are convinced you should have received an increase but didn't get one, you can take your most recent W-2 form to your local Social Security office and ask them to refigure your benefit.

And Finally ...
What To Do When Someone Getting a Social Security Check Dies

Not very long ago, I received a very poignant email from a woman named Maria. She was 85 years old. Jose, her 89-year-old husband of 61 years, was in a hospice. She wrote to me in mid-June and said he probably only had a few days to live. She wanted to know how to handle her Social Security matters after Jose died. Specifically, she told me she was concerned about what happens with their Social Security checks, whom she has to notify at the bank, how she obtains death certificates and what she has to do to claim widows benefits.

I answered Maria directly. But to help countless other wives, husbands or other family members in a similar situation, I will end this book by explaining what happens when someone who was collecting Social Security benefits dies. Many of the points I will make were covered in prior fact sheets, but I will summarize them here.

The first issue we will cover is what to do with the Social Security checks for the deceased. And to do so, I must start out making two points. First, Social Security checks are paid one month behind. So, for example, the check you get in February is the benefit payment for January.

Second, Social Security benefits have never been prorated. This lack of proration can help when someone first starts getting Social Security. For example, if you took benefits at age 66, and you turned 66 on June 28, you would get a check for the whole month of June, even though you were only 66 for three days of the month. On the other hand, if your spouse dies on June 28, you would not be due the proceeds of that June Social Security check, even though he or she was alive for 28 days of the month.

So, I told Maria that when Jose dies, the Social Security check received for that month has to be returned. For example, let's say that he passes away on June 28. That means the Social Security check he might get in July has to go back to the government.

You'll notice I said the check he "might" get. I added that qualifier because there is a very good chance the last check won't even show up in the deceased's bank account. As you may have heard, there are all kinds of computer-matching operations that go on between various government agencies and banks. So, if the Social Security Administration or Treasury Department learns of someone's death in time, they won't even issue the benefit. Or, if the check was issued, the bank will likely intercept the payment and return it to the government before it even hits the checking account. In other words, you usually don't have to worry about returning any Social Security checks. It's almost always done for you.

There can be a little twist to this scenario, though. For example, let's say that Jose dies on July 2. Because he was alive the whole month of June, that means Maria is due the money from that June check that's paid sometime in July — but after Jose died. Once again, there is a very good chance that check won't show up in the bank account because either the SSA or the Treasury Department won't send it or it was issued and the bank sent it back. The difference between this scenario and the first one I described is that Maria is due the proceeds of that check. And it will eventually be reissued to her. More about that in a minute.

But first, a word about getting a death certificate. Maria worried about that. Death certificates are usually issued by city, county or state bureaus of vital statistics. You can frequently get help with this from the funeral director who will be handling the deceased's remains. I told Maria that I was sure her funeral director will arrange to get her copies of the death certificate. But there is even a chance your local Social Security office may not need a copy of the death certificate. They may get proof of death from other sources, such as directly from the funeral home or the bureau of vital statistics.

And speaking of the Social Security office, let's now turn to how you deal with them. Normally, I'd suggest that you try to handle your Social Security business online. But as I've pointed out in Fact Sheet No. 5, a claim for widows or widowers benefits must be done in person. And you do that by calling the Social Security Administration at 800-772-1213. You can either arrange to file a claim by phone, or you can make an appointment to do so at your local Social Security office.

And what you need to do with the Social Security people depends on several factors. If you are just a friend or family member reporting the death of someone who is not your spouse, then all you are really doing is making sure the Social Security checks are stopped. As explained below, the one-time $255 death benefit is not payable. (It can only be paid to a spouse.)

But if you are the spouse of the deceased, then what you do depends on the kind of benefits you were receiving before your spouse died. If you were getting just a spousal benefit (in other words, you didn't have enough work credits to get your own Social Security benefit), then the process is pretty simple. No widow(er)s application is required. You simply notify the SSA of the death, and they push a few buttons to switch you from spousal benefits to widows or widowers benefits.

That was the case with Maria. And because she was well over full retirement age, she will just start getting whatever Jose was getting at the time of death. (However, if Jose started his Social Security at age 62, Maria will actually get a little more. He would have been getting a rate equal to 75% of his full benefit, and as explained in Fact Sheet No. 5, a widow of her age is guaranteed to get at least 82% of her husband's full benefit.)

If you are a spouse who was getting your own retirement benefits, then you have to file an application for widows or widowers benefits. It's not very hard — just a few questions about you and the deceased. You may have to provide a copy of your marriage certificate.

Whether you have an automatic "push button" claim or a formal application, you will start getting widow(er)s benefits effective with the month your spouse died. As I told Maria, if Jose dies on June 28, she will be due widows benefits for the whole month of June, even though she was a widow only three days of the month. Or if he died in early July, she would get widows benefits for July, and she will get the proceeds of Jose's June check issued to her.

And finally, there is the matter of the one-time $255 death benefit. I am always embarrassed talking about this benefit because it is so insignificant. It has a long story too convoluted to get into here. But the bottom line is this: It's been set at the $255 rate for many decades now. Congress occasionally makes attempts to eliminate it. But senior citizen groups get on the bandwagon and keep it alive. So, it has never gone away. But it has never gone up either. Maybe in the 1960s, $255 paid a major portion of funeral costs. But today, it barely will pay for the flowers. Still, it is there to be had. It used to be paid to essentially anyone who applied for it. But about 30 years ago, they changed the law to say the one-time $255 death benefit can only be paid to a spouse who was living with the deceased at the time of death (or to any minor children).

○ ○ ○

Acknowledgments

I would like to thank the team at Creators Syndicate for their help in producing this book, especially Alessandra Caruso and Simone Slykhous.

o o o

About the Author

Tom Margenau worked for 32 years in a variety of positions for the Social Security Administration before retiring in 2005. For many years, he was the director of the SSA's public information office at the agency's headquarters in Baltimore. In that post, he was the chief editor for more than 100 informational publications produced by the SSA.

He also was the SSA's deputy press officer for several years, serving in that position as a chief spokesman for the Social Security Administration. Prior to that, he was a speechwriter for the Commissioner of Social Security. Before he moved to the SSA's headquarters, he worked for 12 years in Social Security field offices around the country, where he processed Social Security claims while writing Social Security columns for local newspapers.

He has been writing his column, "Social Security and You," for national syndication since 1997. Margenau graduated from the University of Wisconsin in 1971. He is married and has two grown children and five grandchildren.

o o o

SOCIAL SECURITY: SIMPLE & SMART
is also available as an e-book
for Kindle, Amazon Fire, iPad, Nook and Android
e-readers. Visit creatorspublishing.com to learn
more.

o o o

CREATORS PUBLISHING

We publish books.
We find compelling storytellers and
help them craft their narrative,
distributing their novels and collections
worldwide.

o o o

Made in the USA
Coppell, TX
22 December 2020

46950696R00066